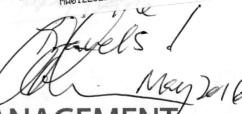

AGILE
PROJECT MANAGEMENT
A Nuts and Bolts Guide to Success

First Edition

ANTHONY C. MERSINO,

PMP, PMI-ACP, CSP, PSPO

VITALITY
CHICAGO

Vitality Chicago
197 Latrobe Ave
Northfield, IL 60093
www.VitalityChicago.com

Vitality Chicago
197 Latrobe Ave
Northfield, IL 60093
www.VitalityChicago.com

To Norma – thanks for all the laughs!

Contents

Acknowledgments

Writing this book was different. In my previous books, I toiled alone to get the work done. With this book, I had a terrific team supporting me and reviewing my work and that made a huge difference in the quality of the end product. It was also a lot more fun, and more appropriate for a book on Agile.

Two people that made significant contributions as reviewers were David Gonzalez and Tom Cagley. David was usually the first person to read and comment on each chapter as I made it available. His perspective as a project and program manager was very helpful. Tom Cagley also reviewed and provided his views as an Agile Coach and a thought leader in software development. Thank you both!

A number of others contributed valuable insights. Sam Siegel applied his Agile experience and editorial background to identify a number of unclear or inaccurate items. Malena Zamora offered personal insights and identified areas that were not as clear as they needed to be. Steve Pasek brought deep Agile knowledge and a sense of humor to the project. A number of others read and provided feedback including Audra Lawlor, Andy DeMarco, Tushar Patel, Greg Brown, Mike Lane, Kevin Ruane, and Janet Gedwill.

Dick Riederer did an amazing job in his editorial review. I envy his keen eye and his proficiency in the nuances of the English language. He was fast and efficient.

Finally, I need to acknowledge the support provided by my home team. They gave me space and allowed me to focus on writing. This included Krista, Jack and of course my wonderful wife Norma. You guys were awesome!

Thank you all very much!

Anthony

x

About the Author – Anthony C. Mersino

Anthony Mersino is an Enterprise Agile Consultant and Coach focusing on driving Agile adoption, introducing Agile techniques, coaching Scrum Masters and Teams, delivering training and supporting Agile at Scale. He helps drive organizational change and builds business value through the adoption and support of Scrum and Agile through the enterprise.

Since 2008, Anthony has been teaching and coaching on applying Agile methods. He teaches several Agile courses for Northwestern University and client companies. He has also supported Agile Transformations at Wolters Kluwer, Riverstar Software, Highland Solutions, Hayneedle, Northern Trust, Redwood Trust, The Carlyle Group, and Bank of America/Merrill Lynch. He has trained hundreds of people to adopt Agile and he coaches teams, Scrum Masters, Product Owners, and leaders and executives.

Anthony is also a recognized expert in soft skills and relationship building. He is the author of the first book ever written specifically to help project managers apply emotional intelligence, *Emotional Intelligence for Project Managers*. Anthony's 28 years of successful project management experience on multi-million dollar projects has taught him what research has shown as well: the emotional intelligence of the project manager contributes more to project success than any other factor.

Anthony has an undergraduate degree from Michigan State University, and earned his M.B.A. from Loyola College in Maryland.

Anthony is a member of the Project Management Institute and the Scrum Alliance. Anthony has been a PMI certified Project Management Professional (PMP) since 1995, a PMI Certified Agile Practitioner (PMI-ACP) since 2012, a Certified Scrum Professional (CSP) since 2015, and a Professional Scrum Product Owner (PSPO) since 2015..

You can read more of Anthony's insights on Agile Project Management on his weblog at: **http://vitalitychicago.com/**.

Other Books by Anthony C. Mersino

Agile Project Management for Teams – Prodevia Learning, Distance Learning Course

Agile Project Management for Teams provides traditional Project Managers, PMO Leaders and Program Managers the practical Agile concepts and techniques required for project success. Students will develop critical Agile skills that are immediately applicable in the professional project environment while also building skills that are increasingly marketable in a very competitive employment marketplace. Designed to provide traditional project managers a useful Agile toolkit, this course includes many real-world examples to assist in its application for Agile project initiative.

Emotional Intelligence for Project Managers; The People Skills You Need to Achieve Outstanding Results

Research indicates that emotional intelligence (EI) accounts for an astonishing 70-80 percent of management success. Technical expertise just isn't enough anymore: project managers need strong interpersonal skills and the ability to recognize emotional cues in order to lead their teams to success. "Emotional Intelligence for Project Managers" introduces readers to all facets of EI and shows how emotions can be leveraged to meet project goals. They'll learn how to: set the tone and direction for the project; communicate effectively; motivate, inspire, and engage their team; encourage flexibility and collaboration; deal productively with stress, criticism, and change; establish the kind of high morale that attracts top performers; and more. The second edition includes several expanded sections on self-awareness and self-management, as well as a new chapter on using EI to lead Agile Teams and a close look at Servant Leadership. Without the people skills necessary to lead effectively, even the most carefully orchestrated project can fall apart. This indispensable guide gives project managers the tools they need to create winning teams and get the job done right and on time.

Emotional Intelligence for Project Managers – Prodevia Learning Distance Learning Course

Emotional Intelligence for Project Managers provides a pragmatic formula for leading project efforts by emotionally engaging project stakeholders. This course provides a down-to-earth, functional method for delivering your own emotional intelligence quotient (EQ) as well as interacting with others at their own EQ level.

Emotional Intelligence for Project Managers can help you:

- Develop stakeholder relationships, a positive work environment and high team morale
- Anticipate and avoid emotional breakdowns
- Leverage emotional information to make better decisions
- Deal with difficult team members, manage conflict and communicate more effectively
- Cast a vision for the project that will attract, inspire and motivate others

Introduction

Over the last decade, Agile techniques have grown in prominence. In fact, so many organizations have experimented with Agile that nearly everyone has either tried it or heard from others who have. And with anything new comes change and resistance to change. Agile seems to have created two camps – ardent followers and those who are opposed to it.

There are many reasons I have heard for opposition; Agile won't work for us, nothing new under the sun, doesn't provide benefits. On the other hand, there are lots of success stories with Agile so I think there is something to be learned from that.

Having a long experience with traditional project management and program management, I can empathize with traditional PMs and their reluctance to embrace agile. Traditional project management is about trying to manage the unmanageable – time, cost and scope. A significant amount of experience, good and bad, went in to the creation of a project management body of knowledge. The intent of the PMBOK is to provide a set of best practices that can be tailored to the situation at hand.

Though I was first exposed to Agile in 2003, I've only been working, studying, applying and teaching Agile techniques since 2008. In the process, I've had to unlearn some things and embrace concepts that were very different than my previous experience as a project manager. I've also found that many of the challenges I felt as a project manager were addressed better by Agile techniques, especially when it comes to managing uncertainty and providing predictability.

This book is intended to help project managers, developers, managers and other team members who are familiar with traditional methods to understand Agile concepts and techniques and be able to apply them when the situation warrants their use.

Why This Book

There are many books about Agile on the market and very few that are targeted to or address project managers. In fact, the average PM is likely to be bewildered by the volume and variability of the information that is available. The books that are available vary widely in quality, scope and practical application. I've referenced several of them for this book. The cited materials in Appendix B and the Scrum Master recommended reading in Appendix C provide more information for further exploration of this topic.

Likewise, there are few training opportunities for a project manager trying to get up to speed. PMI's introduction of the Agile Certified Practitioner (PMI-ACP) certification was an attempt to bring Agile to project managers. I've taught the PMI-ACP preparation training course and it is just a flood of information that the participants need to know in order to pass the exam.

The intent of this training book is to help project managers better understand Agile methods so that they can apply them successfully.

The book is a mix of theory and practical application, with a fair number of real world examples and stories throughout. There is no one size fits all with Agile. Also, Agile is new enough that the idea of best practices is a few years off. Rather, there are examples where good practices might work in a particular situation. Where possible, I've incorporated both and offered my explanation for why things did or did not work out.

Project success rates, at least for IT projects, have been rather low over the years. There are several reasons for the low success rates including faulty assumptions, poor requirements, treating plans as certainty in uncertain environments and holding project managers responsible for unrealistic goals. Unfortunately, we often ignore these underlying causes.

Agile practices address some of these underlying causes by fundamentally changing the way project work is completed. It is no surprise then that Agile projects are 3X more likely to succeed than traditional projects. (Cohn, 2012)

Agile means many things to many people

One of the objectives is to help readers understand the Agile landscape. Agile is an umbrella word that encompasses other concepts like Lean, Kanban and Iterative and Incremental Development. It has also been misused to describe organizations that follow no methodology or chaos. For these reasons, Agile has come to mean many different things to people.

For example, some think of Agile as synonymous with Scrum, the predominant approach. You can be Agile without using Scrum. But so many companies are implementing Scrum that they treat Agile and Scrum as the same thing. They aren't.

Rich History

While to many, Agile is considered a radically different way of doing things, it really isn't. At the heart of Agile is iterative and incremental approaches, rather than plan driven development. Modern Agile incorporates key elements of Lean from the Lean Manufacturing techniques perfected by Toyota, cross functional teams used for new product development and Iterative and Incremental Development used for software development since the 1970s.

By understanding the roots of Agile, project leaders can better understand and leverage these concepts for successful project outcomes.

Agile Means No Project Managers

Perhaps you have heard that teams that are using Agile don't need a project manager to manage them. The teams are self-organizing and they work together to get done what needs to be done. This can be tough for traditional project managers to accept.

Some Agile proponents seem to have a religious or militant leaning, and make a big deal out of this. One of the most popular Agile methods, Scrum, is clear that there is no role for project managers. Further, the role of "Scrum Master" on a Scrum team is so different from a traditional project management role that Scrum proponents don't believe that traditional PMs can function in that role.

This thinking – we don't need project managers – is popular with many even outside Scrum. And right off the bat many project managers get alienated about Agile and tune out without really understanding what it is all about.

I think that is a mistake and my background as a long time PM helps me understand and empathize with them. Rather than being threatened by Agile, PMs can embrace it, understand it and exploit it for their benefit and the benefit of their organization.

In my experience, most organizations find that they do need some form of project management. It doesn't look the same though – it is actually more of a program manager role. The program manager helps coordinate multiple agile teams and align for coordinated releases. Otherwise, there isn't really a project manager who manages an Agile team. In fact, the term Agile Project Manager would be considered an oxymoron to many people familiar to Agile. We will look more at the role of Agile project or Program manager in Chapter 1: *Introducing Agile Project Management*.

For this reason, "Agile project leader" is a term I prefer to use over Agile project managers. Agile project leader can include the aforementioned program manager, a Scrum Master, or pretty much any other member of the team.

The Agile Manifesto

Agile really came into its own back in 2001. That is when many of the thought leaders in software development got together and drew up the Agile Manifesto, a set of 4 Agile values and 12 Agile principles. These values and principles are where the rubber meets the road, so to speak. Mastering these 4 values and 12 principles will serve those who are trying understand and internalize the Agile concepts.

PMI-ACP

In 2011, PMI piloted a new certification, and one not directed squarely at project managers or project management candidates. The PMI "Agile Certified Practitioner" certification, or PMI-ACP was released for general use in January 2012. Since then, it has become the 3rd most popular PMI certification after the PMP and CAPM. More people have the PMI-ACP designation than the Scheduling and Risk certifications put together, even after only less than 2 years.

Pursuing the PMI-ACP is a pretty good challenge. The breadth of knowledge needed for this spans many topics. There were 11 books that were used to develop the exam material and students preparing for the exam should read all 11. However, this particular book is not designed to be a PMI-ACP prep course. While the materials covered are closely related to the recommended reading list for the PMI-ACP, there are many topics on the PMI-ACP that just are not sufficiently covered in this book.

Who is this book for?

This book will appeal to a wide variety of individuals. It is primarily directed at those people who are on technology projects, but it can still appeal to others.

- Traditional project managers or program managers who are interested in applying Agile Techniques for their teams.
- Team members who will be moving to Agile at some point in the future, or who are already using Agile but have not been trained on it.
- Individuals who are interested in preparing for and taking the PMI-ACP Exam.
- Individuals who are stakeholders to agile teams
- Executives and Leaders who are responsible for agile teams.

I've worked with many individuals who are learning about and transforming to agile teams and I never tire of watching the light bulbs go on and see it click for them. My hope for you is that you will also internalize these concepts, and then put them to work for your success. One thing I like about Agile is the expectation that you are always examining your outcomes, learning from your experience and striving to continually improve. I hope you will throw yourself fully into this work.

My own Agile Background

I've been working as a project manager since the late 1980's, and I have been focused on Agile since 2008. However, my first exposure to Agile was in 2003. At the time, it wasn't called Agile- it was just the way that the developers on my team chose to get work done. I recall that it was focused, and it brought the developers together with common objectives, yet it provided individual team members with autonomy.

Since 2008 I have worked directly with a dozen different organizations who hired me to help them move from traditional development to Agile. It is really exciting to witness teams go through the process of adopting Agile. They tend to be so much more productive, engaged and satisfied with their work. I love working as an Agile coach and seeing this process.

I have also engaged with hundreds of others who have attended my training courses, or that I have met at Agile Meetups. I have heard their stories – positive and negative – about the process. It is easy for one person to change, but much more difficult to change an entire organization. I am not naïve about what it means to be a change agent and to help individuals, teams and companies change.

My Agile training courses have been primarily centered on those development teams who are making the transition to Agile, and teaching them how to productively develop solutions. I've also taught the PMI-ACP certification training to project managers, Agile overview courses for executives and leaders and advanced Agile and Scrum techniques to Scrum Masters I was coaching. To prepare me for teaching, I found both the Certified Scrum Master Training, and the PMI Agile Certified Professional Training to be helpful. I've also had the opportunity to learn from some great Agile thought leaders through training courses, their presentations at conferences and their published works. By no means do I think I have arrived – learning Agile is a process and something I expect to continue for quite some time. I hope you will join me in this endeavor.

Kind Regards,

Anthony Mersino

Chapter 1: Introducing Agile Project Management

Introduction

Congratulations! You are one of many people today who are exploring or deepening your understanding of Agile methods. Likely you hope to understand and leverage Agile to make your teams and project more successful. Perhaps you are a stakeholder of an Agile team and you'd like to better understand some of the terms they are using. Or, you may be in a position to join or lead an Agile team and you want to prepare yourself for that. These are all great reasons to want learn more.

As we will see, Agile is different from traditional development and project management approaches. What works for Agile projects may not work for traditional ones, and vice versa. Don't worry, this book is going to make it easy to understand Agile and add Agile tools to your toolkit!

Key Takeaways for Chapter 1

By the end of Chapter 1, you will be able to:

- Describe Agile and clarify what it is, and what it is not
- Understand Key Agile Terminology including Agile Project Management
- Understand what being an Agile Project Manager means

- Compare traditional projects to Agile projects and understand some of the key differences

Defining Agile

I am a little surprised when students arrive to my courses without an understanding of just what Agile means in the context of projects or software development. Agile continues to grow in popularity and it seems that most project managers would have at least heard of it. Perhaps the term "Agile" has been overloaded to the point where it has lost its meaning. So let's start by defining Agile and related terminology. Where it makes sense, we'll draw a distinction between Agile and traditional project approaches.

Let's start by taking a little quiz to see what you think of Agile. Please record your answers to the following question:

What is Agile to you?

1. A new software development method
2. The silver bullet
3. Iterative & Incremental Development
4. Anything you want it to be
5. Many things to many people

OK, I can admit that this is a bit of a trick question. In some cases, Agile represents all of these things. Let's talk them through one at a time and see which answers are correct, or mostly correct.

1. Is Agile a New Software Development Method?

Is Agile a new software development method? Perhaps. Agile includes software development methods, like Dynamic System Development Method (SDM) or Crystal Methods. The predominant use of Agile is for software development, though it has been successfully applied to many other business processes, and even entire organizations. As we will see shortly, the roots of Agile are in Lean *Product* Development and the Toyota Product System. So I think answer 1 is not completely accurate.

2. Is Agile a silver bullet?

The idea of finding a silver bullet that would solve all the problems that ail software development was thoroughly explored by Frederick Brooks in his famous book, The Mythical Man Month. In it, Brooks responds to the pursuit of others in his profession to find a 'silver bullet' that would solve the problems of large scale software development, saying:

"There is no single development, in either technology or management technique, which by itself promises even one order-of-magnitude improvement within a decade in productivity, in reliability, in simplicity."

Frederick Brooks (Brooks, 1995)

Since writing his book back in 1975, Brooks has found himself repeatedly ignored. Organizations continually strive to find some secret tool or technique to solve their complex problems with software development. And it is the teams who suffer. Who hasn't lived through the introduction of Computer-aided Software Engineering (CASE) Tools, Prince, Lean Six Sigma, CMMI, or any of the other myriad approaches that were going to solve the problems with technology projects? If you have a PMO, fire them. If you don't have a PMO, start one.

I've heard this phenomenon accurately called the "Shiny Object Syndrome", or organizational Attention Deficit Disorder (ADD). Managers, desperate for some kind of quick fix or miracle cure, try out new methods, hoping that the next one will make the difference they need.

Indeed, many people today treat Agile as the next Silver Bullet, though it most certainly is not. "Going Agile" may not solve your current problems and could actually introduce a lot of new ones. Agile could help focus your teams, or provide a basis for quickly responding to change.

3. Is Agile Iterative and Incremental Development?

Well, yes. Agile does rely on iterative and incremental development methods. They were not new with Agile – as we will see in Chapter 2, those methods have been around since the 70's and earlier. In fact, incremental development was one of the promising approaches that Fred Brooks mentioned in his 'no silver bullet' chapter.

Agile does imply iterative and incremental development (IID), but it is broader than that. So it does not equal IID.

4. Is Agile Anything You Want it to Be?

Absolutely! Many people treat Agile as anything that they want it to be, or use the term as a shield to deflect criticism or transparency, while they do whatever they want. I've been to organizations where they perform some Agile ceremonies, like a daily standup, and they call themselves Agile. But unfortunately that was the only Agile practice they did, and they met sitting down and it took them an hour. That doesn't sound very Agile.

Others use the term Agile as an excuse to avoid any type of documentation (rather than only what is necessary) or practice ad hoc (aka sloppy) development techniques. They've created their own definition of Agile and use it to avoid being grown up, professional software developers.

5. Is Agile Many Things to Many People?

This last choice, many things to many people, is probably the best answer. This is partly because Agile is an umbrella term that includes many different things, including Kanban, Lean and Scrum. It is also because the term is so widely used, and misused, that by itself it doesn't mean much.

Let's dig in on what it means to be Agile, explore some of the facets of Agile and leave you with a clear understanding so that you can comfortably converse with others who claim to be Agile. Let's start with some definitions.

Agile Defined

Webster defines agile (agile with a small "a") as:

"Marked by a ready ability to move with quick easy grace", and "mentally quick and resourceful".

In the context of technology teams, Agile software development is:

"A group of software development methods based on iterative and incremental development, where requirements and solutions evolve through collaboration between self-organizing, cross-functional teams. It promotes

adaptive planning, evolutionary development and delivery, a time-boxed iterative approach, and encourages rapid and flexible response to change. It is a conceptual framework that promotes foreseen tight interactions throughout the development cycle". (Anon., 2014)

The term Agile was coined by the early software development thought leaders as a way to contrast their ideas with the waterfall approach that was common practice at the time. The waterfall approach was considered 'heavy'; heavy with process and heavy with documentation. The software development thought leaders wanted something that was light. To draw a sharp distinction between what they were doing and waterfall, these thought leaders began using the terms 'light' and 'lightweight'. Eventually they settled on 'Agile' at a meeting in Utah in 2001, when they wrote the Agile Manifesto.

What is Agile Project Management?

Agile project management is difficult to define, as we will see shortly. So let's start with some other definitions that are a little easier.

Project

The definition of a project is pretty well established. The Project Management Institute (PMI) defines a project as:

"A temporary endeavor undertaken to create a unique product, service, or result."

It's important to note the focus here on temporary and unique. PMI drives the point home in this elaborating statement:

"The temporary nature of projects stands in contrast with business as usual (or operations), which are repetitive, permanent, or semi-permanent functional activities to produce products or services. In practice, the management of these two systems is often quite different, and as such requires the development of distinct technical skills and management strategies." (Project Management Institute, 2008)

What PMI is saying here is that projects are different than ongoing, repetitive processes, and the activities needed to produce products. And this is one of the first challenges that project managers are going to run into when they want to be Agile, or join an Agile team. The temporary and unique nature of projects is somewhat incongruent with Agile. Agile teams are not temporary; Agile teams strive to stay together indefinitely. Additionally, the idea of doing something unique is handled differently in Agile. Rather than treat the team activities as unique, we treat them as a steady stream of repeatable activities. In this sense, Agile teams and Agile projects (if you want to put these terms together), look a lot more like product development than project management. In fact, the roots of Scrum are based on new product development as we will see in Chapter 2.

Project Management

PMI defines project management as "the application of knowledge, skills, tools and techniques to project activities to meet the project requirements." That is also a straightforward definition.

Agile Project Manager

So how do we define an Agile project manager? Consider the following question:

FIGURE 1.1 – WHICH OF THESE EXIST?

Clearly there is no Easter Bunny or Santa Claus. I argue that there is no such thing as an Agile project manager. The trainers from the Scrum Alliance agree with me. When we look closely at Scrum later in the book, we will see that all the roles of a traditional project manager are taken on by the team or by the business owner for the team. The idea that we would have one person who would plan, coordinate the work of others, manage tasks and report status for the team just doesn't fit with being Agile.

Please don't send me hate mail justifying your value as a project manager, or telling me that every project needs a project manager to be that single point of accountability. I get it. Agile is not anti-project management at all. It is just that Agile helps us organize our teams to reduce management overhead, and it puts the accountability for results on those individuals who are in a position to impact those results. Additionally, most PM experience and individual skills are out of alignment with the style of servant leadership needed on Agile teams.

The point I am trying to make is to not fight for the importance of a PM role in an Agile environment. Rather, I advise project managers to understand Agile and play a role that adds the most value. There are some discrete roles for project and program managers on Agile teams and we will look at those later in this book. Project managers can participate on Agile teams though they may need to change their approach to maximize the value that they bring to an Agile team.

Agile Projects

As you might have guessed, the idea of an Agile Project is something of an oxymoron. Agile can be used for projects, but it is a bit of a misuse. The concept of a project in Agile is quite different from what traditional projects look like. And individuals wouldn't be "Agile" on one project, and then leave and be not Agile on another. It is not so much a methodology as a mindset.

I am not sure that there is a definition for an Agile Project. I've researched this for a while and have yet to find a good definition for an Agile project.

You would think that Jim Highsmith, author of **Agile Project Management**, would include a definition for "agile project" in his book; he doesn't. The closest thing I could find to a definition for agile project is from Doug DeCarlo, author of **Extreme Project Management**. DeCarlo defines an extreme project as:

An extreme project is a complex, high-speed, self-correcting venture during which people interact in search of a desirable result under conditions of high uncertainty, high change, and high stress.

(DeCarlo, 2004)

To give you a better understanding of the difference between a traditional and an Agile project, consider the following example.

Imagine you are going to print a newsletter for your company (I know, I am dating myself). This is a one-time thing to support a major product launch. You and your team write out the content, someone generates a PDF, someone else takes it to a printer and they print it. You have a newsletter. What I just described is a project – it is unique and temporary.

Now consider the printing of daily newspapers like the Chicago Sun Times. Content is written for the paper every day. Every day it goes to the printing presses. Sunday editions are pulled together, produced and delivered. The same teams work together seamlessly to produce the output – a newspaper. The content inside is unique, but the final product that sits on the newsstand looks pretty much the same. This type of work looks a lot more like Agile.

Agile Project Management

Sanjiv Augustine, author of **Managing Agile Projects**, defines Agile Project Management as:

"the work of energizing, empowering, and enabling project teams to rapidly and reliably deliver business value by engaging customers and continuously learning and adapting to their changing needs and environments." (Augustine, 2005)

Wikipedia lists Agile Project Management:

Agile management or Agile project management is an iterative and incremental method of managing the design and build activities for engineering, information technology, and new product or service development projects in a highly flexible and interactive manner, for example Agile software development. (Wikipedia, n.d.)

Have I thoroughly confused you now? I've been looking at this for a couple of years now and I have confused myself. There is a lack of standardization around these terms. Some people believe that placing "Agile" in front of something makes it, well, Agile. The term has become diluted and ambiguous and it fails as a descriptor. And putting Agile and Project together is incongruent.

Many organizations seem to be confused as well about the people they need to help them with Agile. Quickly glancing at some job postings I see the following three: Agile PM/Scrum Master, Senior Agile Project Manager, Project Manager / Scrum Master. What exactly do those titles mean?

Complex Adaptive Systems

Another term that you may hear in relation to Agile teams is Complex Adaptive Systems. Before we dive into the definition, let's describe something that we are probably all familiar with that is not a complex adaptive system.

I love to cook, and that is probably because I like to eat. (I like to eat so much it borders on addiction, but let's not go there right now.) There is nothing I would rather do on a weekend than pick a food that I love, find a recipe for it online, shop for the ingredients and then make it. I am thrilled that most any recipe I can imagine is out there and readily available on the internet. Do you love the Turkey Chili from Deer Valley? That recipe is out there. How about the lasagna from Maggiano's? That is out there as well.

FIGURE 1.2 A GREAT RECIPE

And the beautiful thing is that by just following the steps in the recipe, I can make food as good (or nearly as good) as what I would have at the restaurant. It is just me cooking, there is very little magic that I bring as the cook, and the results are highly predictable.

FIGURE 1.3 – FOLLOWING A RECIPE

Wouldn't it be nice if running our projects were just like following a recipe? We would just follow all the steps in the recipe until we have a delicious outcome at the end. That is the fallacy of traditional, plan-driven projects. The thinking is that if we have the right plan (recipe), and we follow the steps carefully, we will have a great outcome. Unfortunately, things are not that simple; there are too many variables.

In fact, most of traditional project management boils down to variance management, which is continually comparing plan to actual to determine the variance. Project management is largely trying to reduce or eliminate that variance. We erroneously believe that if we could just get our results to conform to our plan, then we would succeed. "On Time, On Budget, On Scope" is our mantra. But what happens when our plans are flawed, unrealistic, or don't lead us to valuable outcomes for the project stakeholders?

Unfortunately, most software projects cannot be run like a recipe. Technology projects and new product development teams fall into what is called complex adaptive systems.

Complex adaptive systems are made up of independent actors and forces that make predictability nearly impossible. One can control the inputs, but one cannot control the independent actors who will be part of the project.

Sanjiv Augustin, author of *Managing Agile Projects*, describes complex adaptive systems as:

Living systems such as projects are complex in that they consist of a great many autonomous agents interacting with each other in many ways. The interaction of individual agents is governed by simple, localized rules and characterized by constant feedback. Collective behavior is characterized by an overlaying order, self-organization, and a collective intelligence so unified that the group cannot be described as merely the sum of its parts. Complex order, known as emergent order, arises from the system itself, rather than from an external dominating force. These self-organizing Complex Adaptive Systems (CAS) are adaptive in that they react differently under different circumstances and co-evolve with their environment.

(Augustine, 2005)

When dealing with a complex adaptive system, sticking to the plan is a recipe for failure. Rather, empirical process control is employed. What this means is that the results of the process are monitored and the process is changed or adapted until it produces the desired results. In the context of a team it means we monitor the results we get at the end of every iteration or timebox, then we adjust the process to get the desired or improved outcomes.

Revisiting the triple constraint

I remember well my introduction to the triple constraint, back in 1993. I was taking on a new job with the official title of project manager, and I took an introductory project management course from the American Management Association. I learned that for any project, there is a relationship between the scope, timeline and the cost. A change in any one of these constraints will cause a change in one or both of the others.

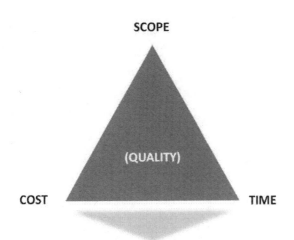

FIGURE 1.4 – THE TRIPLE CONSTRAINTS

The triple constraint made sense to me as soon as I heard about it. Of course there is a relationship between scope, cost and time for every project. And if we want the project to go faster, it will cost more or you may have to cut some scope. An experienced co-worker of mine used to quip, "Good, fast, or cheap, pick any two."

The only thing was, I had another co-worker Dave who didn't know about the triple constraint. In the late 1980's, I worked with Dave as part of an engineering team at IBM. Dave had been tasked with managing a project to consolidate one data center into another, to reduce costs. He had done this type of project before. For various reasons, he chose to accelerate this project schedule to hit a particular critical date. He had teams working 3 shifts a day instead of just one shift. He accelerated the timeline, AND, to my surprise he also beat his budget. WHAT? What Dave discovered was that even though there was no reduction in scope, he was able to save money by cutting the timeline. So how was he able to do this?

Well, it seems that by getting things done sooner, there were certain run rate costs that were reduced. There was also a greater sense of urgency which kept everyone focused. The premium Dave paid for the contractor to provide teams that would work around the clock to accelerate the move, was less than his savings in project run rates. And the stakeholders loved it!

That insight from so many years ago was like a loophole in the law of the triple constraint. The iron triangle was not as rigid as I had been led to believe. And since then, it always had me wary that I might be missing something, that there might be a better way. And there was. In 2008, when I really began researching Agile projects, I saw that better way. And it is not a loophole.

With traditional projects, the 3 constraints of scope, cost and schedule are fixed. Usually this starts with determining and fixing the scope, and then estimating the time and cost to deliver on that scope. With the scope fixed, the teams are allowed (usually) to vary the timeframe and the cost. Those 3 constraints form the basis for our plan in a traditional project.

Unfortunately, we've learned that scope is almost never fixed; it tends to change over the life of the project. The development team and the customer often learn things that change the scope, or the competitive landscape changes. As the scope changes, our original cost and time estimates are going to be impacted.

Agile projects turn the triangle upside down. In Agile projects, cost, time and quality are fixed. We leave scope as the variable constraint. We know when we will be done, and how much it will cost, but we don't know how much will be done. The scope is allowed to vary – we get as much done as we can in the timeframe for the budget. This is often shown by 'flipping the triangle' of triple constraints as shown by the triangle on the right in the diagram below. We know the cost of the project – that is the weekly run rate of the team. Since we have fixed the time frame, we can use that to calculate an overall cost and schedule. What we don't know, is what will be delivered at the end.

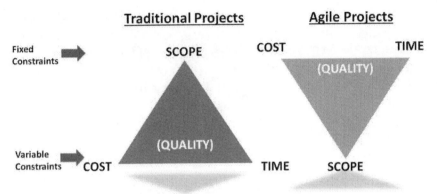

FIGURE 1.5 – THE TRIPLE CONSTRAINTS OF TRADITIONAL AND AGILE PROJECTS

One other subtle difference is the treatment of quality in Agile projects. In traditional projects, quality is not openly considered or discussed and unfortunately quality is the first lever that teams pull when they cannot meet their dates. The triple constraint ignores quality, though experienced professionals will talk of it as a fourth constraint. Teams cut corners on development and testing to meet the dates, and wind up with spaghetti code that is costly and difficult to maintain. They create what is called technical debt.

With Agile teams, Quality is supposed to be a fixed constraint. Agile teams have a standard for what constitutes "done" for their team which means all the tasks necessary to make it potentially shippable. They don't cut corners on getting something done. They don't throw it over the wall to another team to do testing or integration, they do it all. They also use tools like test driven development (TDD) and Acceptance Test Driven Development (ATDD) to make sure that the right item is developed, and it is developed correctly. Agile teams sometimes do cut corners unfortunately, but the framework is there to support them to do their best.

Why do we need Agile? What problems are we trying to solve?

Many traditional project managers seem defensive when I talk to them about Agile. I sometimes feel like I am evangelizing or selling them on Agile. They will often ask me "What is the problem we are trying to solve?" Maybe they hope that they won't have to change, or that a Jedi mind trick will shift the focus away from them.

We could certainly accept that things are good enough, but I challenge you to think in terms of continuous improvement. Everything can be improved. Is your company leading your industry, or are there competitors who are faster, cheaper or just better? If we aren't striving to improve and get better at what we do, we will fall behind.

Craig Larman is a world class expert in scaling lean and agile development. I had the opportunity to get 3 weeks of training and coaching from Larman as part of a large Agile transformation at a major financial services firm. One of the interesting things that Larman shared about Lean manufacturing techniques that were invented at Toyota was that a frequent goal for lean organizations is to outlearn the competition. Business today is competing on a global level. If you are not moving forward, advancing and getting better, then you are likely falling behind. I know that may sound stressful or uncomfortable, but unfortunately it is true.

"Outlearn the competition."
-*Dr. Allen Ward* (Larman & Vodde, 2009)

In the world of technology projects, things are and have been broken for a long time. To illustrate my point, let's take a look at project success rates for software development and technology projects. Though this particular discussion focuses on software development projects, there are applications to other types of projects.

The Chaos Studies

The Standish Group has been studying technology project success rates for the last 20 years. Starting in 1994, the Standish Group surveyed project successes and failures every two years and published their results in what has become known as the Chaos Studies.

The Standish Group uses the triple constraint as their measure of success. Projects that met the original plan were considered a success. That means they were delivered on the original schedule, within the planned budget, and with the planned functionality or scope. Projects that missed on any one of the triple constraints were considered "challenged". And those projects that missed on two or three of the constraints were considered failures.

Based on this definition, project success rates have gone from horrible to just poor over the last 20 years. The chart that follows shows project success rates over the last 18 years. (Standish Group, 2012) In the first year of the study (1994), only 16% were successful. In the most current year, 37% were successful, which represents a 50% increase in success rates. But even with that improvement, there are still 2 in 3 projects that are not considered successful. This is pathetic! What other field would tolerate a success rate of 1 in 3? Brain surgery? The airlines? Food service? Airline food service? This is the problem we are trying to solve! We can and must do better.

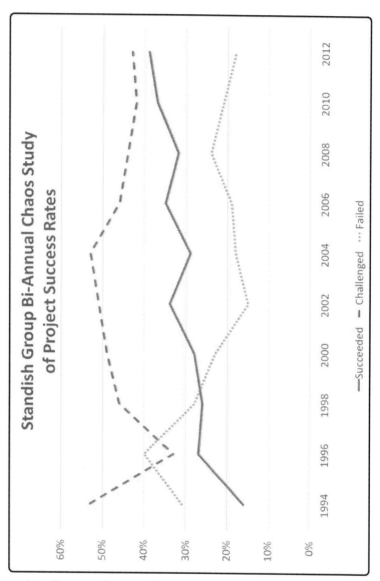

FIGURE 1.6 – PROJECT SUCCESS RATES

The Chaos Studies have their critics, to be sure. The critics challenge the success measures and the definitions. Many people feel the Standish Group approach is flawed, that there is too much focus on living up to the original estimates which may or may not be correct. I tend to agree. Estimating is tough work, in particular for projects where the team has little or no experience. That doesn't change the facts that based on the Standish Group and project management standards for success, 2/3 of projects are not successful.

Why Projects Fail

Whether we use the Standish Group Chaos Studies or other success measures, we generally agree that success rates, at least for IT projects, are low. Too low! There are many reasons that have been given for low success rates that have been documented over the years. Some of the most common reasons for failure at the project level include:

- Unrealistic, faulty, or overly optimistic assumptions
- Poor understanding of requirements, or rapidly changing requirements
- Sticking to the plan, even when the plan is based on faulty assumptions and changing requirements

There are also some environmental or systemic issues that negatively impact many or most projects. In my experience, these systemic issues go unnoticed or unchallenged. Even though they also have a huge impact on the success rates for projects, they are either ignored, or they are viewed as system constraints that cannot be changed. All organizations suffer from these issues to a greater or lesser extent.

- **Taking on Too Many Projects** – In many organizations, the project review and approval process results in most or all projects getting approved, even though the projects cannot be completed with the resources available. Rather than making a "go/no go" decision, many organizations have a new project review process that results in a "go/go go" decision, as one of my students described it. Organizations seem to be unable or unwilling to prioritize projects, and they say yes to projects that they don't have the capacity to complete. This results in unrealistic expectations for all projects. Too many projects are started, and then organizations juggle resources to try and keep all stakeholders happy. The focus shifts to the stakeholder who is screaming the loudest.

- **Over-allocation of People** – Partly as a result of the previous item, team members are assigned to multiple projects in an attempt to get everything done as promised. Additionally, PMOs and resource managers mistakenly believe that resource allocation is equivalent to productivity, so they strive to make sure that everyone is 100% allocated (or more). They load everyone up with multiple projects. "Busy is good" is the thinking. Rather than having slack or buffer, we load people up and virtually wipeout thinking and creative time. Individuals end up serving many masters, and always question "what is the highest priority". "Just tell me what to work on" is a common refrain from them. (Research single piece flow for more on this topic.)

- **Constantly Changing Priorities** – Often in response to the items above, the focus and priority is shifting constantly. Organizations seem to have ADD (Attention Deficit Disorder). They change direction and priorities frequently and leave teams with throwaway work. Or, they lack the ability to make decisions so the teams are left with doing nothing, which is never a good idea.

- **Constant Interruption** – This fourth item is about the constant interruption of developers and other creative people, causing context switching. This is a downstream impact from the previous three items. By assigning people to multiple high priority projects, we force them into a mode where they are shifting gears all day. This context switching has a cost. Tom DeMarco and Timothy Lister estimate that creative people need 15 minutes on average to get back into a creative state of mind after an interruption. (DeMarco, 1999) The more projects a particular person is assigned, and the more changes in priority, the higher the loss of productivity.

I bring up these last four problems because it has only been through my exposure to Agile that I have begun to see how crazy this approach is. I had seen these challenges over and over, but just thought they were the only way that things could be done. Now I have learned the ways that Agile teams overcome these challenges.

These problems are not new. Project management and software development thought leaders invested a lot of time and effort trying to overcome these problems. And that is where Agile comes in. In Chapter 4, we will dive into Agile and begin to explore how it will help. I don't want to imply that Agile teams won't face these problems, they will. But Agile teams have tools to help reduce the risk of these challenges.

Key Differences of Agile Projects

It should be pretty clear to you by now that I am a huge fan of Agile. I think you will be too, after you finish with this book. Here are some of the key aspects of Agile that I really like, and I want you to be on the lookout for. They highlight some of the key benefits of Agile methods, and how they relate to some of the areas of concern I had when leading traditional projects. I hope that you will find them useful as well.

1. **Communications** - Most of us would agree that communication is an important, if not critical part of successful projects. Traditional projects tend to focus on communications that provide a document trail, or protect us in case something goes wrong. We send emails to confirm conversations; we record decisions and changes for the primary purpose of knowing who to blame later if things go wrong. By contrast, I like the less formal and more intimate forms of communications that Agile teams use. I like the frequent and focused daily team communications that occur during the short daily meetings that Scrum teams use. I also like the concept of pairing (2 people working together) from XP; it helps share knowledge and build stronger teams. Finally, I have a strong preference for using the most intimate communication mode available, face to face meetings, rather than email.

2. **Transparency** - Organizations benefit from teams that are clear about their progress. A recent study of PMO leaders showed that 58% didn't believe that project managers provided accurate status reports; the PMs were misrepresenting the true status of the projects they managed. (Visitacion, 2011) You probably have seen this for yourself. There are those projects that are green right up until the due date and then they are red when they miss their go live date. There are also watermelon projects – those that are green on the outside but red on the inside. It doesn't need to be this way!

Agile team status and progress is typically posted in a public place, displaying clear progress against plan, with nothing hidden and no surprises. Updates are often daily, but at least weekly or at the end of the sprint. And the PM is no longer responsible for acting as the agent between the team and the customer or management. On Agile teams, the people working on the tasks are responsible to provide clear and transparent progress reporting at the person-task level, rather than the project manager running around and collecting the information. Agile tasks are granular enough that they get done by one person in about a day or less. Task reporting is tracked to one of three states: "not started", in progress or done. Teams don't waste time trying to guess what is the % complete for a task, deliverable, or project.

Another subtle point about progress reporting is that teams only report task status to their own team members, there is no one else who needs or uses the information. External progress reporting is done at the working software level.

3. **Predictability** – I've worked on a lot of traditional projects and it was rarely possible to predict with any certainty when things would be completed. I've seen too many projects where it was on time right up until the date for launch or go live, and only then was it late. Those are unwelcome surprises! If you don't have accurate forecasts, it's not working!

   Technology projects are complex and unpredictable. By contrast, Agile teams have fast and effective ways of estimating the work remaining and when the overall project will be completed. The teams use the actual delivery of working software (i.e. velocity) as a predictor and they track it on a weekly or bi-weekly basis.

4. **Short Cycles** – I've been on large scale projects and programs that spanned multiple years. These long time frames led to a number of issues; lack of focus or sense of urgency, snow-plowing work to future phases, and unpredictable timeframes and costs. Agile teams break work down into short iterations of 1 to 4 weeks. Each short cycle produces something of value to the end user or customer.

5. **Constant Feedback and Learning** – The main tool for learning on traditional projects was the post-mortem at the end. Lessons learned at the end of the project are frequently an exercise with low return on investment. Who reads those or acts on the lessons learned from the end of a project? By contrast, Agile teams incorporate feedback on a regular basis. Each day there is often a point of reflection, and a regular team retrospective (structured lessons learned) occurs at least every 2-4 weeks.

6. **Planning, and Re-planning** – There is an old project management saying that we "plan the work and work the plan." There is an assumption that if we can plan it, we can deliver it. The truth for many types of projects is that they are just too complex to be able to plan and deliver.

    Some of the best teams I have been on have adopted rolling wave planning to deal with this challenge. With rolling wave planning, teams plan in detail only the work that is immediately in front of them, and they spend less time planning work that is in the distant future. Agile teams leverage rolling wave planning to defer planning in detail until the last responsible moment.

7. **Adapting to Change** – One of the main reasons that companies are adopting Agile today is because of the pace of change. It is a highly competitive landscape and most companies are under pressure to deliver faster and faster and to be able to pivot and change direction in response to customer needs or competitive pressure. Agile teams are able to leverage change so that it is not disruptive; in fact, it is welcomed by the team and incorporated into the regular work routine. Agile teams also expect that they are able to incorporate what they are learning and leverage that to change.

8. **Requirements** - For all but the smallest of efforts, it is impossible to state with accuracy the requirements up front. It may actually be counter-productive to specify them in detail, based on the previous point about change and learning that occurs during execution. Our methods need to flex, to recognize this fact. And if the requirements cannot be known well in advance, we should not spend a lot of time on developing detailed budgets and schedules to complete those requirements. Let's stop pretending we can accurately schedule things that are unknown and unpredictable.

9. **Accountability and Commitment** - The project manager has been thought of as the 'single throat to choke', or 'the first one to take a bullet when the team fails'. The reality is that it takes an entire team (oh my, I almost said "it takes a village"). The team, not the PM, can either deliver a successful project or not. To that end, we need mechanisms to shift the accountability and commitment to the team members.

10. **Self-Organizing Teams** - It is more efficient for the team to figure out what needs to be done, and execute it, than for a project manager to tell the team what to do. It is also more humane, and more satisfying for the team members. A key Agile principle is that the best solutions come from self-organizing teams.

11. **Minimizing Unnecessary Work** – One of the 12 Agile Principles is about simplicity and maximizing work not done. Agile provides a framework that helps make unnecessary work visible, allowing teams to make decisions about reducing or eliminating it. Continuous and close engagement with the customer, eliminating multi-tasking or context switching and reducing documentation deliverables are just a few examples of steps that can be taken to reduce unnecessary work.

Chapter 1 Summary

- Agile is a mindset change; a shift in the way we look at work
- Agile methods grew out of new Product Development and a desire to improve software development to make it more "light" in process and documentation, and to improve project success rates.
- Agile is very different from traditional project management. The characteristics that define a project – unique and temporary – are in conflict with Agile thinking. This makes Agile projects and Agile project management a bit of an oxymoron.

Chapter 2: A Brief History of Agile

This section provides a detailed look at the origins of Agile. It will help you understand and appreciate Agile thinking and principles, however, you may choose to skim or skip over this section if you want to get to the Agile Values covered in Chapter 3.

Key Takeaways for Chapter 2

By the end of Chapter 2, you will be able to:

- Provide a brief history of Agile, including some of the Agile techniques that are not commonly used today
- Provide context and background for modern Agile approaches

The Genesis of Agile

In Chapter 1, we talked about waterfall development and the view that it was heavy with process and documentation. We also talked about the rate of failure for technology projects. These two factors drove various software development thought leaders to attempt to improve tools and methods, and reduce risk and failure. Agile wasn't born in a vacuum.

Agile also wasn't born in a single day, and it wasn't created recently. A number of separate events occurred that resulted in Agile becoming a mainstream approach to software development. The timeline below shows some of the key milestones in the history of Agile; each will be described briefly in the paragraphs that follow.

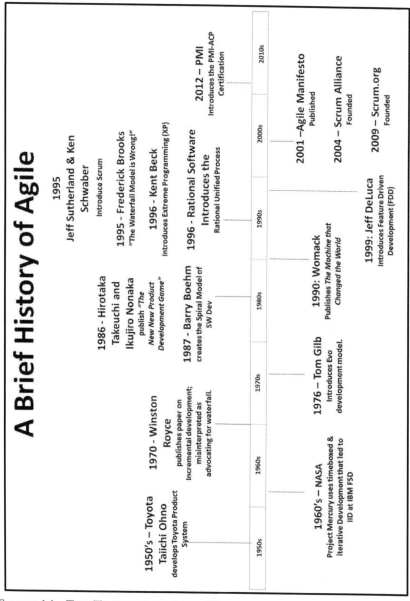

FIGURE 1.1 – THE TIMELINE OF AGILE HISTORY

Iterative and Incremental - NASA's Project Mercury (1960's)

The timeline above shows the evolution of Agile methods, stretching all the way back to the use of iterative and incremental methods on NASA's Project Mercury. Those early experiments were a precursor to additional Agile-like approaches used at IBM's Federal Systems Division. (Larman, 2004)

What is meant by iterative and incremental? Iterative development is about getting a working version out, and then enhancing and creating improved versions usually with the input of customers or end users. Goat path is an approach that exemplifies this approach. A goat path is a minimal version supporting an activity in its simplest form. The next version might be considered a gravel road, then a paved road, etc. We don't build the paved road first – it would take too long and without customer validation we don't know exactly what is required.

And that is a benefit of iterative approaches – you don't need to have clearly defined requirements up front as you would with waterfall. This enables you to begin development sooner on the most well understood or highest priority requirements. Teams often choose the most risky requirements as a starting point – to reduce risk and fail fast, if failure is what will happen. Teams get early working solutions that can provide look and feel to the customer, and requirements are expected to evolve. Rework is likely with the iterative approach.

With an incremental approach, the team develops one small part of the solution at a time, and delivers in small chunks. Imagine you are building a wall, one brick at a time. Similar to the iterative approach, development on a small chunk can start early, before all the requirements are completed for the other chunks. This can be useful to get an early look and feel, and helps to reduce risk by identifying dead ends or blind alleys.

Iterative and incremental approaches are commonly used together in Agile methods. A common abbreviation for Iterative and Incremental Development is IID.

Royce Accidentally Invents the Waterfall Method (1970)

One of the more ironic events in Agile history was the release of the 1970 paper, "Managing the Development of Large Software Systems", by Dr. Winston Royce. In this paper, Royce explored various methods of software development and recommended an approach that leveraged iterative and incremental development.

He also outlined the linear and sequential approach that later came to be called Waterfall development, though he noted that this approach was "risky and invites failure". His writing was taken out of context and the waterfall approach became the norm for most software development over the next 30 years and is still the standard for many organizations. (Royce, 1970)

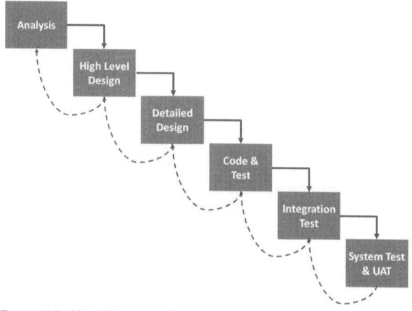

FIGURE 2.2 – THE WATERFALL APPROACH

The Waterfall approach gets a lot of bad press these days and I don't think all of it is deserved. It has been used for many years, and sometimes it was very successful. I've used it successfully for large projects and programs. It works best on projects where the requirements are well defined up front, and not subject to change. Because development is sequential in one single pass, the Waterfall approach is best suited to projects that have been done before such as building a spec home, or upgrading servers.

Things have changed over the years and fewer projects have stable requirements or have been done before. Most projects I am involved with today are using new technology have evolving and uncertain requirements. I was taught to use aggressive "change control" to manage or prevent change. Unfortunately, that mechanism often led to conflict with the customer, and inhibited them from getting the system they needed.

The waterfall method makes sense from an intellectual point of view. It is logical and step by step. We will write down everything we need to do in each phase, and then we will do it. "Plan the work, work the plan" describes this line of thinking. I think it appeals to most project managers who believe that with the right plan, we can accomplish nearly anything.

Barry Boehm – Spiral (1986)

I first ran across Barry Boehm's Spiral model of development when teaching project management courses for ESI International in the early 2000's. It was intriguing to me, though I completely misunderstood the intent of the model. Like many people, I saw it as a linear, waterfall development method that repeated. It wasn't. It was a method of iterative and incremental development that included aggressive prototyping and a focus on risk analysis and reduction. It makes sense in the context of iterative and incremental development. The U.S. Military has leveraged the Spiral approach as outlined in DoD directives 5000.1 and 5000.2.

The New New Product Development Game (1986)

A 1986 article from the Harvard Business Review had a deep influence on Jeff Sutherland, the co-creator of Scrum. The article "The New New Product Development Game" looked at innovations in new product development and how some teams were able to innovate faster than others. Authors Hirotaka Takeuchi, Ikujiro Nonaka looked closely at these teams and found that they were highly empowered and cross functional. Takeuchi and Nonaka identified the following nine characteristics of the high performing teams that they dubbed "Rugby Style". (Takeuchi, 1986)

- **Autonomous** – The teams had a great deal of autonomy over the way that they were managed.
- **Transcendent Goals** – The teams had large goals that transcended their individual jobs.

- **Cross Fertilizing** – The team members were expected to cross train each other to develop strong cross functional skill and knowledge.
- **Built-in Instability** – Management gave the teams large challenging goals which forced teams out of their comfort zone.
- **Self-Organizing** – Beyond the large goals, teams were left to themselves to figure out what to do to accomplish the goals.
- **Overlapping Development Cycles** – Rather than follow a linear path through analysis, design and development, these teams found themselves doing all of these activities in parallel.
- **Multi-Learning** – The team members learned as much about their environment, the company products and the environmental constraints as they could.
- **Subtle Control** – Subtle control was given to the teams by giving them large challenging but very clear goals. It was up to the team to do whatever was in their power to accomplish the goals.
- **Organizational Transfer of Learning** – The teams were responsible for training others in the organization on the products and knowledge they developed.

As we will see in the discussion on Scrum, these nine characteristics had a significant impression on Jeff Sutherland when developing Scrum.

The Machine that Changed the World (1990)

In the mid-1980's, a team from MIT led by James Womack began studying the global automotive industry. They looked at how Lean manufacturing approaches, such as the Toyota Production System, were replacing the widely used mass production techniques that were first pioneered by Henry Ford. Those companies who continued to use those mass production techniques to gain efficiencies of scale, were finding those same approaches inflexible, slow to respond to changes, and ultimately wasteful and costly. (Womak, 1990)

One of the most significant findings of the MIT studies was the approach to the labor force. The automotive companies used layoffs as a way to manage their labor needs, which fostered low trust. Plus, the highly specialized and highly repetitive nature of the work in automotive assembly plants was boring, demeaning and led to low worker motivation and a lack of care. Management and workers were frequently at odds with each other as workers and unions fought for higher wages and less work.

Toyota used a different approach, in part because of the environmental factors that faced it as an early company. Their treatment of their workers is probably one of the most important differences. Toyota treated the labor force as a fixed investment and guaranteed them employment for life. They chose to invest heavily in educating and developing the workforce, and to treat them as one of the most important assets in the organization. It wasn't just lip service – Toyota counted on the workers to think, to learn and teach others and to innovate. Workers typically were organized into teams that were responsible for a variety of tasks so cross-training was important. The managers understood the jobs the best and taught and served the workers in their department.

Womack and his team went on to write 3 other books on this topic. Their work led to Lean Software Development as well as to Lean Six Sigma and ultimately influenced Agile.

The Waterfall Method is Wrong (1995)

For so long, the waterfall approach was the standard for software development in organizations. Frederick Brooks is the author of the well-known "Mythical Man Month" first published in 1975. He named his keynote presentation for the 1995 International Conference on Software Engineering, "The Waterfall Method is Wrong" and that seems to have summed up his thinking.

The Birth of Scrum (1995)

Jeff Sutherland invented Scrum in 1993 when he was the Chief Engineer at Easel Corporation, working on the fourth generation programming language that became Object Studio. He had been studying best practices and read literally hundreds of papers before he read the aforementioned New New Product Development Game. (Sutherland, 2 Apr 2012)

Sutherland first put Scrum to work at Easel Corporation. He created the roles of Product Owner and Scrum Master and hired people to fill them. He also created the first Product Backlog and delivered working products with it. Sutherland partnered with Ken Schwaber in 1995 to formalize the Scrum process and together they delivered a paper on it at the OOPSLA'95 conference.

The Birth of Extreme Programming (1996)

They say that necessity is the mother of invention, and that seems to be the case for Extreme Programming or XP. In 1996, Kent Beck became the project leader of the Chrysler Comprehensive Compensation (C3), a payroll system for Chrysler Corporation. As was the case for many large-scale software development projects at the time, the project was over budget and way behind schedule, and seemed to be doomed for failure.

Beck needed to get something done and fast. He pulled together his best programmers and chose to focus the team on using a set of software development practices that were unconventional at the time, like test-first development and pair programming. These practices came to be known as XP and were first documented in Beck's book, Extreme Programming Explained, which was published in 1999.

XP has matured over the years and the list of technical practices is currently about 20. Though XP can be used by itself, it is not a methodology or framework, it is just a set of practices. Many Agile teams use some or all of these technical practices in combination with frameworks like Scrum. We will look at XP in a little more detail in Chapter 4.

The Birth of FDD and Adaptive Software Development (1999)

Feature-Driven Development

Feature-Driven Development (FDD) was developed by Australian Jeff De Luca, based on a lightweight framework he had been experimenting with for years. It was first described in Chapter 6 of the book, *Java Modeling in Color with UML* by Peter Coad. Later it was codified in *A Practical Guide to Feature-Driven Development*, published in 2002.

FDD is based on a set of five processes. The first process is to develop an overall model, which is a high-level overview of the system and its context. Additional detailed models are developed if needed.

The second process is to build a feature list, based on the models. The third process is to plan by feature, resulting in a high level development plan.

The fourth and fifth processes are to design by feature, and build by feature, respectively. These two processes make up nearly 80% of the effort of the project. Based on the high level development plan, each feature is designed and then built. Completed features are then incorporated into the main build.

Adaptive Software Development

Adaptive Software Development (ASD) was created by Jim Highsmith and Sam Bayer, based on rapid application development techniques they had been using since the early 1990's. A key component of ASD is the lifecycle comprised of three steps – Speculate, Collaborate and Learn. The term speculate was intentionally chosen for what would traditionally be called planning, and the point was that most plans are simply that – speculation. Highsmith repeats this approach to planning in his book on Agile Project Management, as we will see in Chapter 5 on Planning Agile Projects.

ASD shared ideas with other early Agile methods including feature based, short timeboxed iterations and responsiveness to change. (Highsmith, 2002)

Others

There were a number of other Agile-related initiatives that are not shown on the timeline. Though not as well-known as the others, each of these made some contribution to the growth of Agile as we know it. These include Rapid Application Development (RAD), DSDM, Lean Development, Unified Process and Crystal Methods.

Rapid Application Development (RAD)

In the early part of the 1990's, Rapid Application Development (RAD) was introduced. RAD was based on iterative development and extensive use of prototypes. RAD was developed as an alternative to Structured Analysis and Waterfall methods which were considered inadequate or unsuitable since they didn't accommodate changing requirements or rapid delivery.

Unfortunately, there was little agreement on exactly what was or was not RAD. For more information, see *Rapid Application Development* by James Martin, or *Rapid Development* by Steve McConnell.

Dynamic Systems Development Method (DSDM)

DSDM is an iterative development model that originated in England in 1994 and is still popular in Europe today. It grew directly out of the RAD movement and was an attempt to provide structure and standards while still delivering working systems in less time. DSDM focuses heavily on the human element of software development, believing that most projects fail because of people issues.

Lean Development

Lean Development was the application of those lean manufacturing concepts and principles identified in the 1990 Womack book, *The Machine that Changed the World: The Story of Lean Production,* to the development of software. Bob Charette was one of the main thought leaders for Lean Development in the early 1990s. He viewed Lean Development as a strategic, top-down initiative that included the entire organization and not just the technology group. The measurable goal of Lean Development is to build software with one third the human effort, one third the development hours and one third the investment of traditional (SEI CMM) organizations.

With the publication of *Lean Software Development: An Agile Toolkit* in 2003, Mary and Tom Poppendieck have extended Lean Development into a formal framework. We will look at Lean Software Development in more detail in Chapter 4.

Unified Process

The Unified Process grew out of the Unified Modeling Language (UML) developed by Ivar Jacobson, Grady Booch and James Rumbaugh, who became affectionately known as the "Three Amigos". UML led to the creation of the Objectory Process in 1988. Objectory was purchased by Rational Corporation in 1995, and the Rational Unified Process was introduced in 1996. The three amigos published *The Unified Software Development Process* in 1999.

The Unified Process was based on the following 6 best practices for software development:

1. Develop iteratively, reducing risk
2. Manage requirements
3. Employ a component-based architecture
4. Model software visually
5. Continuously verify quality
6. Control changes

In 2003, Rational was bought by IBM and the process has been renamed or rebranded several times over the years to include Agile Unified process, Open RUP, Essential Unified Process and other variations.

Crystal Methods

Crystal Methods was developed by Alistair Cockburn, one of the signers of the Agile Manifesto. Cockburn places a high priority on communication and conversation, in fact, the title of his book on Agile Software Development includes the subtitle, "The Cooperative Game".

Crystal evolved in to a set of scalable methods. The simplest was Crystal Clear, a lightweight method originally designed for one team of up to 8 developers, working in the same location. Crystal Yellow, Orange, Orange Web, Red, Maroon, Diamond and Sapphire represent approaches that scale based on size and criticality.

Key ideas that Crystal and Alistair Cockburn contributed to Agile include frequent delivery of usable code, reflection and process improvement, osmotic communications and barely sufficient. Osmotic communications occur when teams are co-located and sitting close together. Each team member can selectively tune in and out of conversations, so that knowledge is shared across the team. Barely sufficient is a phrase used to describe not doing any more work than is necessary. For example, Agile teams produce documentation that is barely sufficient.

The Agile Manifesto (2001)

The story of the Agile Manifesto is pretty widely known among Agile enthusiasts. Seventeen of the thought leaders on software development met in Snowbird, Utah for work and play. They compared notes about the things that each of them were working on. Most fell into the category of lightweight methods – the light being oppositional to the heaviness that most of them had experienced while working with the waterfall or plan driven development. They wanted to focus on people, collaboration and flexibility. They wanted to avoid heavy documentation and heavy process.

The outcome of the meeting was an agreement on 1) a new term for their collective approaches (Agile), 2) a set of four values for software development, and 3) a set of 12 principles. While the participants didn't agree on everything at the detail level, they did agree at the level of the values and principles. These values and principles continue to be relevant and they guide Agile teams everywhere even today. We will look more closely at the Agile Manifesto in the next section.

Founding of Scrum Alliance (2004)

Ken Schwaber founded the Scrum Alliance with Esther Darby and Mike Cohn in 2004. Primarily a training and certification body, the Scrum Alliance helped to promote the growth of Scrum. The Certified Scrum Master (CSM) was the first designation, which was easily obtained with only classroom training. The Scrum Alliance also offered the three more rigorous certifications, the Certified Scrum Practitioner (CSP), Certified Scrum Product Owner (CSPO) and Certified Scrum Trainer (CST).

Founding of Scrum.org (2009)

Ken Schwaber left the Scrum Alliance and founded Scrum.org in 2009. His stated goal was to strengthen Scrum, improve the profession and to introduce training and certification programs for Scrum Developers. Scrum.org provides Professional Scrum Master (PSM), Professional Scrum Developer (PSD) and Professional Scrum Product Owner (PSPO) assessments and certifications.

PMI Introduces the PMI-ACP Certification (2011)

It is against this backdrop that the Project Management Institute (PMI) decided to introduce the Agile Certified Practitioner (PMI-ACP) designation. As the primary certification body for project managers across the globe, PMI has a major stake in how Agile projects are run. PMI's interest in Agile was seen as recognition that Agile methods are more than a passing fad.

Rightly or wrongly, Agile had become viewed by many as an alternative to project management, or as an alternative to plan driven project management approaches. It's not really accurate to view it as one or the other, though many do. Interestingly enough, the PMI-ACP designation is not directly targeted to project managers. You don't need to be a project manager to get the certification.

In 2011 PMI began to pilot the PMI-ACP. After a pilot group of just over 500 in 2011, PMI launched the certification in January of 2012. Since then, the PMI-ACP has gone on to become the fastest growing PMI certification. As of December 31, 2013 the PMI-ACP has outgrown the previous three certifications introduced by PMI as shown in the chart below. (PMI, 2015)

Certification	Designation	Launch	Active Holders (Nov 30, 2014)
Project Management Professional	PMP	1984	639,023
Certified Associate in Project Management	CAPM	2003	25,060
Agile Certified Practitioner	PMI-ACP	2012	6,987
Risk Management Professional	RMP	2008	2,966
Scheduling Professional	PMI-SP	2008	1,254
Program Management Professional	PgMP	2007	1,131
PMI Professional in Business Analysis	PMI-PBA	2014	192
Portfolio Management Professional	PfMP	2014	168

FIGURE 2.3 – THE RISE OF CERTIFICATIONS

Chapter 2 Summary

- Agile methods grew out of new Product Development and a desire to improve software development to make it more "light" in process and documentation and to improve project success rates.

Chapter 3: Agile Values and Principles

Key Takeaways for Chapter 3

By the end of Chapter 3, you will understand:

- The Agile Manifesto including the Values and Principles
- The Agile "Declaration of Interdependence", and some of the key values for Agile leaders that will be used throughout this book

The Agile Manifesto

The now famous 2001 meeting of 17 software development thought leaders in Utah resulted in the Agile Manifesto. If you visit the Agile Manifesto site you will see the graphic below. (Cunningham, 2001)

FIGURE 2.1 – THE AGILE MANIFESTO

The 17 signers of the Agile Manifesto are, for the most part, still active in software development. Many of them went on to innovate, to teach and write books and to continue to advance Agile in organizations. You will see many of their names listed in the citations and bibliography.

The Manifesto is made up of 4 values and 12 principles which are explained in the sections that follow.

Agile Values

The Agile Manifesto lists the Agile Values as follows:

> We are uncovering better ways of developing software by doing it and helping others do it. Through this work we have come to value:
>
> | Individuals and interactions | over | processes and tools |
> |---|---|---|
> | Working software | over | comprehensive documentation |
> | Customer collaboration | over | contract negotiation |
> | Responding to change | over | following a plan |
>
> That is, while there is value in the items on the right, we value the items on the left more.

Source: http://agilemanifesto.org/

FIGURE 3.2 – AGILE VALUES

These 4 values are the core of Agile thinking. Let's take a closer look at each of these values.

Individuals and Interactions over Processes and Tools

People are important. Jim Collins talks a lot about getting the right people on the bus, and the wrong ones off the bus in his book, "Good to Great." (Collins, n.d.) I think that the people who wrote the Agile Manifesto knew at some level that without the right people, projects cannot succeed. The right people and how they interact, are at the heart of any successful project.

The contrasting value, 'processes and tools' are also important, they are just not as important as people and interactions. This contrast is deliberate. Nearly every organization I have worked in since 1993 was focused on their methodology, or, how to get things done. I personally spent hours, days and months working on project management plans – documents that described how projects would be run. These documents ran into the hundreds of pages and spelled out every process to be followed, the roles and responsibilities of the team members and all the deliverables that would be produced by the project. It was a necessary first deliverable of every major project or program. And it was mostly a waste of energy.

There was a push in the 1990's and 2000's toward ISO or CMM/CMMI certification. The idea was, if you had solid processes for how the work was to be performed, pretty much anyone could get the job done. The authors of the manifesto thought otherwise- it isn't about getting just anyone, it is about getting the right people and having them work together. Frederick Brooks wrote that the best programmers are 10X more effective than the average one. (Brooks, 1995)

This first Agile value should prompt some thought. First, what is treated as more important in your organization today, people or process? If you are not sure, look at the policies, rules and rewards. What is the intention and outcome of these organizational constructs?

Next, what would it look like in your organization to place more of a priority on people and their interactions, instead of processes and tools? Rather than investing in CMMI certification, audits, assessments or methodology, what if the organization invested in helping people develop their craft of software development? What if you worked on being an organization known for technical excellence? What if we increased salaries in order to attract and retain the best developers, those that are more productive by a factor of 10?

Working Software over Comprehensive Documentation

This second Agile value is about the importance of delivering working software. Though originally written with software in mind, I think you could also substitute 'working solutions' and apply this to most teams and organizations. The idea here is that value is created when we deliver solutions to the people that need them. It's a pretty simple concept. So why even include it as one of the 4 Agile values?

In the earlier description of the waterfall method, we talked about the sequential, step-by-step approach to delivering software. We don't get around to writing actual code until late in the process. There are other non-software deliverables that document the results of each stage. These deliverables are necessary for a number of reasons. For example, there are frequently different team members working at each stage of the project and they rely on documentation as a handoff. Separate teams may be performing testing and validation. In some cases, contracts dictate the deliverables as protection against getting nothing.

The work of creating documentation can be non-trivial, and sometimes it takes on a life of its own. Take a look at this sample list of deliverables below from a major systems integration project I helped lead in 1998. This was a subset of 30 of the 350 deliverables for this particular phase, for the implementation of a vendor software package. Can you spot any deliverables that are documentation only, and not software?

1. A.CR.010 - Scope, Objectives & Approach (version 2)
2. A.CR.020 - CR Strategies, Standards & Processes
3. DBR005- Requirements Traceability Verification Matrix
4. DBR260- PM Tool - Microsoft Project 98
5. DBR278- Time Reporting System Documentation
6. DBR279- Time Reporting System Support
7. A.CR.030 - Quality Plan
8. A.WM.010- Work Flow Management Strategies, Standards & Processes
9. A.WM.020 - Project Workplan
10. A.WM.030 - Finance Plan
11. A.RM.010 - Resource Management Strategies, Standards & Processes
12. A.RM.020 - Staffing Plan
13. A.RM.030 - Project Organization
14. A.RM.040 - Physical Resource Plan
15. A.RM.050 - Project Infrastructure
16. DBR002- Develop Integrated Logistic Support Plan
17. A.QM.010- Quality Management Strategies, Standards & Processes
18. A.CM.010 - Configuration Management Strategies, Standards & Processes
19. A.RD.010 - Financial & Op Structure
20. A.RD.020 - Current Business Baseline
21. A.RD.030 - Future Process Model
22. A.RD.040 - Future Bus Functional Model
23. A.RD.050 - Process & Mapping Sum
24. DBR264- Requirements Definition for Repository Database
25. DBR272- Integrated PM Tool & AMG Interface Setup
26. A.TA.010 - Architecture Scope, Objectives & Approach
27. A.TA.020 - Architectural Strategy

FIGURE 3.3 – AN EXTREME EXAMPLE OF PROJECT DELIVERABLES

Sadly, none of the deliverables in the list above are working software, they are all documents. And these represent less than 10% of all the deliverables for this particular project!

From a cost and risk point of view, the production of these deliverables early in the lifecycle is a significant investment with dubious return on investment. These documents don't help the end user to do their job, they cost money and they have no value. Further, until we get to the business of writing valuable software and then put that software in the end users hands, we have cost with no benefit. And considering the number of projects that are cancelled outright, we are investing with a distinct possibility of NEVER getting a return.

I can almost hear some of you screaming about your audit requirements and need for system documentation that seemingly cannot be reduced or eliminated. You have decisions to record, and change requests to document. Your QA department needs a complete set of requirements and design documents to build their test scripts. You have to comply with SOX legislation.

What I find is that most of the perceived documentation requirements are actually just a misunderstanding of what is truly required. Most organizational documentation requirements have grown over time. They've become 'the way things are done around here'.

In other cases, the documents support handoffs from team to team and are only necessary because we have structured our organizations in a way that forces handoffs. When we move from silos to cross functional teams, we eliminate the need for documents to communicate.

During Agile transformations with small and large organizations, I frequently sit down with the relevant parties from the PMO, Audit, Quality Assurance, or whomever else is requiring documents. It is in these discussions that we often get to what is truly required. It frequently turns out to be a lot less than most people believe. When you have the right people in the room and you discuss the true requirements, many or most of the perceived documentation requirements go away. When you sit down in a face to face discussion and go over specific documentation requirements, typically the Agile teams meet them without any type of modification.

So think about your own organization and the priorities. Does the organization place a priority on the delivery of working software, or on documentation? Consider having a discussion with the QA manager, or the PMO to go over documentation requirements.

Customer Collaboration over Contract Negotiation

The next value is about customer collaboration. Too frequently I've worked in organizations where there is an adversarial relationship between the development or technical team and the customer. The team thinks that customers never know what they want, or, they always change their mind. It's hard to satisfy or delight the customer, or even meet expectations when the relationship is poor and collaboration is absent.

Obviously customers are what makes projects possible. Without customer problems to solve, and corresponding budgets, there would be no need for software developers. This is a symbiotic relationship. Customers are actually critical to the survival of technical teams. So it makes no sense to not collaborate with them.

The early Agile enthusiasts believed that customers were the key, and that collaborating with customers was more important than contract negotiation. A typical form of contract negotiation occurs on teams as part of the requirements and change process. When you hear things like "that was not in the requirements" or "that change is going to cost you more" then you know you are in the contract negotiation process. Agile teams harness change for the customer's benefit, as we will see when we study the principles. Contract negotiation put us in a low-trust, adversarial relationship with the customer. One side wins, and one side loses.

Responding to Change over Following a Plan

We have talked about the contrast between Agile methods and following a plan. This Agile value reminds us of the need to recognize that change is the constant in all that we do. And it is not that planning is bad – we definitely plan. We just recognize that change is a constant, and we want to be prepared to respond to it.

This idea of responding to change has become even more critical today than it was in 2001 when the authors wrote it. Organizations are competing in a global economy where speed to market and responding to competitive pressures can make or break organizations. Revenue growth and profitability are tied to a company's ability to innovate, to meet evolving customer needs and to meet or exceed competitor offerings.

The corresponding right side value is following a plan. As we discussed earlier, most of project management is about determining where we are off plan and what to do about it. We are not orienting to customer needs and competitive business pressures when we continue to follow a plan that does not address those needs and pressures.

Where Do Project Managers Tend to Focus?

Sadly, I have to say that for most of my career as a project manager, the items on the right were a higher priority for me than the items on the left. I was not a developer, and I did not consider myself a technical person. The tools and processes, the comprehensive documentation, the contracts and following a plan were all the things that I was comfortable with. Delivery of software was not something I could do. I was a non-value add worker, as one of my Agile trainers called it. I gravitated to those things I could master. I suspect many project managers had a similar focus. It is not to say I did not value those things on the left, I just think it was not my primary focus.

The 12 Principles of Agile Development

While I like and appreciate the four Agile Values, I have really come to love and embrace the 12 Agile Principles. They build on the values, and give teams some importance guidance on thinking and behavior:

We follow these principles:

Our highest priority is to satisfy the customer through early and continuous delivery of valuable software.

Welcome changing requirements, even late in development. Agile processes harness change for the customer's competitive advantage.

Deliver working software frequently, from a couple of weeks to a couple of months, with a preference to the shorter timescale.

Business people and developers must work together daily throughout the project.

Build projects around motivated individuals. Give them the environment and support they need, and trust them to get the job done.

*The most efficient and effective method of
conveying information to and within a development
team is face-to-face conversation.*

Working software is the primary measure of progress.

*Agile processes promote sustainable development.
The sponsors, developers, and users should be able
to maintain a constant pace indefinitely.*

*Continuous attention to technical excellence
and good design enhances agility.*

*Simplicity--the art of maximizing the amount
of work not done--is essential.*

*The best architectures, requirements, and designs
emerge from self-organizing teams.*

*At regular intervals, the team reflects on how
to become more effective, then tunes and adjusts
its behavior accordingly. (Cunningham, 2001)*

These principles are so valuable that during my training courses I will have teams teach them to each other or do other exercises to help them understand and internalize the principles.

The Agile Mindset

The 4 Agile values and 12 Agile principles form the basis for what a friend of mine calls the Agile Mindset. The Agile Mindset is a way of thinking that emanates from an understanding of the Values, the Principles, and then any specific methods or approaches one might apply, such as XP, Scrum, or DSDM. These methods and frameworks align with and support the Agile Values and Principles. Figure 3.4 shows what the Agile Mindset might look like.

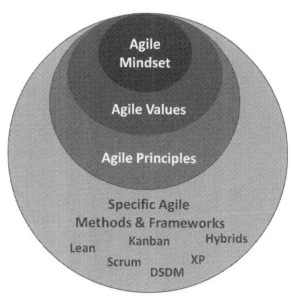

FIGURE 3.4 – THE AGILE MINDSET

The value of the mindset is to align and guide one's thinking. At the highest level is alignment with Agile Values, then the principles, then the specific method or framework being used.

As an example, consider a situation where we have a Scrum team that is co-located. However, there is a manager who is a key stakeholder to the team who worked in another city. The Scrum team is using a physical task board and a burndown chart drawn on a flipchart to track their progress and coordinate their work. (We'll talk more about task boards in Chapter 5; for now reference the picture below.) The manager in the other city couldn't walk by and see the task board or burndown chart. He requested that the team post their burndown chart daily on a SharePoint site. What should the team do? (This example comes from a situation that actually occurred to a team I was coaching.)

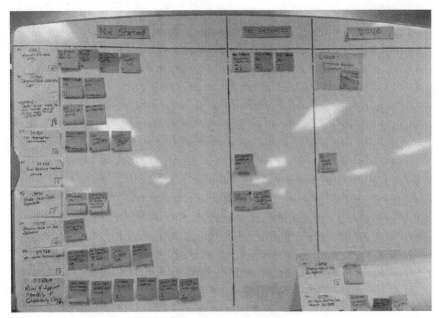

FIGURE 3.5 – A SCRUM TEAM'S PHYSICAL TASK BOARD

In applying the Agile mindset, we start first with the four Agile values. While there is nothing specific about status reporting, the values do put customer collaboration over contract negotiation. Is the posting of a burndown chart a form of customer collaboration? Is the manager a customer? No and no. Another value that should be considered is working software over comprehensive documentation. One might think of the burndown chart as a form of documentation; it certainly isn't working software. Both the task board and burndown chart are team tracking tools that provide visibility to work in the current sprint, and provides an indication of whether it will be completed or not.

Next we would move on to the 12 Agile Principles. Consider "Business people and developers must work together daily throughout the project", does that apply? Not really. What about "The most efficient and effective method of conveying information to and within a development team is face-to-face conversation."? No again.

The principle that I think is most relevant here is: "The best architectures, requirements, and designs emerge from self-organizing teams." Self-organizing teams make their own decisions, they track their own work and they don't need a manager. The burndown chart is a tool that supports team self-organization. If the team wants to share that with the manager, they could, but it is really up to the team to decide. (In the end, the facilitator for the team was able to convince the manager to try getting an update at the end of every two weeks.)

This is just one example of how the Agile Mindset could be used as a lens to look at situations. As Agile leaders, I encourage you to internalize the values and principles, and use the mindset to help navigate challenging situations and conflict. We can also teach and coach our teams to apply the mindset as well.

Agile Declaration of Interdependence

The Agile Manifesto and the story behind it are pretty well known. A somewhat less famous document was developed by another group several years after the Agile Manifesto. Called the Agile Declaration of Interdependence, the document sets forth a project management approach that is compatible with Agile.

Agile and adaptive approaches for linking people, projects and value.

We are a community of project leaders that are highly successful at delivering results. To achieve these results:

We increase return on investment by making continuous flow of value our focus.

We deliver reliable results by engaging customers in frequent interactions and shared ownership.

We expect uncertainty and manage for it through iterations, anticipation and adaptation.

We unleash creativity and innovation by recognizing that individuals are the ultimate source of value, and creating an environment where they can make a difference.

We boost performance through group accountability for results and shared responsibility for team effectiveness.

We improve effectiveness and reliability through situationally specific strategies, processes and practices. (Highsmith, 2005)

The authors of the Declaration of Interdependence included a couple of the original authors of the Agile Manifesto, Alistair Cockburn and Jim Highsmith. Others included David Anderson,

49

Sanjiv Augustine, Christopher Avery, Mike Cohn, Doug DeCarlo, Donna Fitzgerald, Ole Jepsen, Lowell Lindstrom, Todd Little, Kent McDonald, Pollyanna Pixton, Preston Smith and Robert Wysocki.

I am not sure what the authors of the Declaration of Interdependence intended to happen to their work. Perhaps they thought it might become as famous as the Agile Manifesto, I don't know. I haven't run across much.

Something that I have run across and found helpful is a set of Agile Values for Project Leaders. This comes from Jim Highsmith in his book, Agile Project Management. Jim claims that his list of three key values summarizes the values in the Agile Manifesto and the Declaration of Interdependence.

Delivering Value over **meeting Constraints**

Leading the Team over **managing the Tasks**

Adapting to Change over **Conforming to plans**

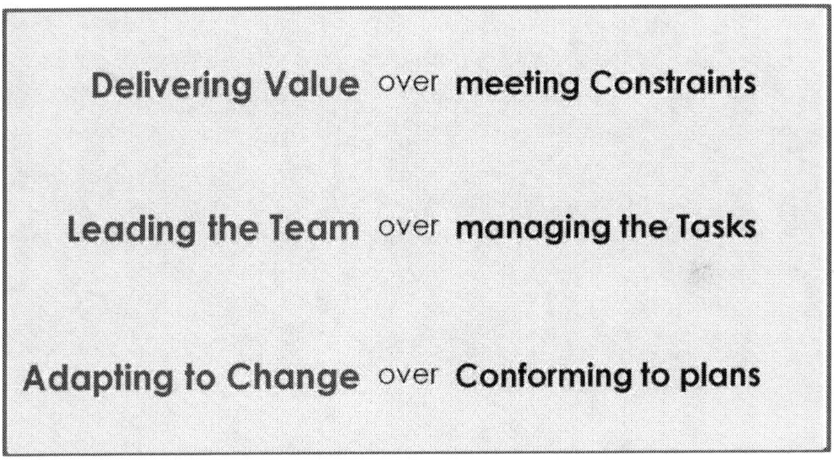

FIGURE 3.6 – AGILE VALUES FOR PROJECT LEADERS (HIGHSMITH, 2010)

I like these values and see the value for those who are in project management or leadership roles. We will look at each of these in more detail in the next section.

Value over Constraints

Delivering value is extremely important for Agile projects, so much so that many of the 12 Agile principles speak to value:

- Principle #1 - Our highest priority is to satisfy the customer through early and continuous delivery of valuable software
- Principle #3 - Deliver working software frequently, from a couple of weeks to a couple of months, with a preference to the shorter timescale

- Principle #7 - Working software (or solutions) is the primary measure of progress.
- Principle #10 - Simplicity--the art of maximizing the amount of work not done--is essential.

As mentioned earlier, Agile projects view the triple constraints of time, budget and scope as flipped from the traditional view. The time and budget for Agile projects is fixed while the scope is allowed to vary. We don't spend any more time than necessary developing detailed project schedules. The budget is simply the time frame multiplied by the run rate of the project. We strive to have stable teams so we don't have people coming onto and off of the team.

Within those fixed constraints of time and money, we focus on delivering the most important and valuable requirements first. If we were to show this as a picture, it might look something like the picture below. We have a prioritized backlog, as represented by the stack of stories or features shown on the left. And on the right, we have a timeline that consists of 5 sprints, each of which results in potentially shippable product increments, or PSPI. We may even have a minimally viable product (MVP) after some number of those sprints, representing something that could be deployed to users.

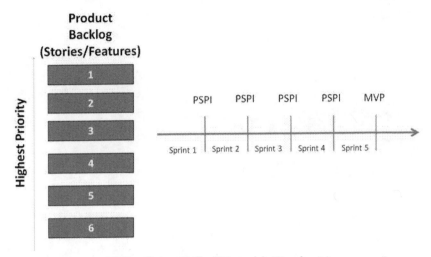

PSPI = Potentially Shippable Product Increment
MVP = Minimum Viable Product

FIGURE 3.7 – THE STARTING POINT FOR DELIVERING HIGH VALUE FEATURES FIRST

The picture above represents the starting point, before any work is done. Where we experience real value is when we make smart decisions about the priorities and deliver only what is needed. In the next diagram, we see that after completing one sprint, we delivered the first 2 features from the list. Based on what we learned in that sprint, we have added 3 new features, and deleted two features that we determined we no longer needed as shown in the diagram below. After just one sprint, we used what we learned to change the scope and direction and reprioritized features to increase the value of what we delivered.

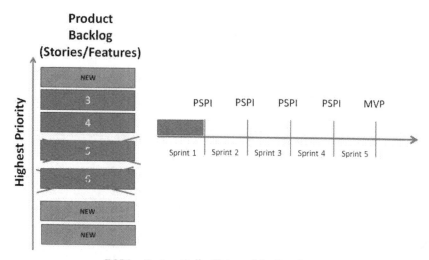

PSPI = Potentially Shippable Product Increment
MVP = Minimum Viable Product

FIGURE 3.8 – CHANGES IN SCOPE AFTER THE FIRST SPRINT

The beauty of this approach is that we might decide that not all the features are needed to ship a minimum viable product. We might decide that a scaled down version is all that is justified in the market.

We might even decide that we need to cancel the project and begin work on something that would have more value. Think about that concept for a moment – that we could decide to cancel the project. If by learning something from an early story, we decide that there are better uses for our investment, wouldn't it make sense to stop immediately? The challenge is, once organizations have a large sunk cost in an initiative, it becomes very difficult to stop and change direction. Agile provides an easy way to do this. In fact, one of the Agile principles speaks to this – maximizing work not done.

"Principle #10 - Simplicity--the art of maximizing the amount of work not done--is essential."

Can you think of any examples of projects that would have been better off **not done** in your environment? What about work not done? Where is there waste in your organization? A short list of software development wastes is shown below and described in more detail in the sections that follow.

1. Partially Done Work
2. Extra Features
3. Relearning
4. Handoffs
5. Delays
6. Task Switching
7. Defects

Partially Done Work

Any type of intermediate work product, any inventory of partially finished work and any code that is not in production is considered partially done, and waste. There is no value in partially done work – value is only realized when solutions are put into production.

To avoid partially done work, work on fewer things at the same time and take them all the way from not-started to either in production or potentially shippable. Eliminate handoffs between teams or within the Agile team. Break work down into small features that can be completed entirely within one sprint. Establish and leverage a definition of done that will apply to all backlog items.

Extra Features

Developing extra features is often called gold-plating. To avoid developing extra features, make sure that you have acceptance criteria for all stories. That criteria should guide the team to develop only what is needed. Leveraging test driven development is another technique that helps guide teams to only deliver what is needed.

Relearning

Relearning is when the teams have to learn again something they have already learned and forgotten. This occurs when time passes between for example specifying requirements, and design and development. Or the time that passes between development of an item and testing and debugging.

To reduce or eliminate relearning, take items all the way from "not started" to complete within one sprint. Avoid any type of handoffs. And leverage small teams (9 or less) of dedicated individuals. Don't spread one person across several teams, no matter how attractive this is or necessary it seems.

Handoffs

Eliminating handoffs have been suggested as the solution to several different wastes. The way to eliminate handoffs is to rely on a dedicated, cross functional team for all development. This Agile team should take items from not-started to done, without relying on other teams.

Dedicated means that this team works only on work for this team, they are not spread across multiple teams. Cross functional means that the team has a primary skillset, such as Python Development, but they also have several secondary skill sets, like testing or analysis. The entire team strives to understand the business environment as well.

It should be clear to you by now that the traditional approach of having different part-time experts perform tasks on a project is not aligned with Agile. It may be hard for traditional project managers to imagine work being done this way, but it really does work. And when you see it working, it actually makes you wonder why you thought the traditional approach was helpful.

Delays

Delays are a killer to any project and they often cannot be anticipated in advance. To avoid delays, identify and remove bottlenecks to your process. For example, if you have just one expert on testing or requirements, have them cross-train the rest of the team. If there is an SME that the team is dependent on, negotiate for their time.

You can also reduce delays by working on one item at time, and taking it all the way to completion. Finally, many teams use a checklist for backlog items, called a definition of ready. They only work on stories in the current sprint that meet the definition of ready, and they spend time in the current sprint making items 'ready' for future sprints.

Task Switching

Task switching is another waste. Every time we shift gears, we lose productivity. So it makes sense to switch gears as infrequently as possible.

I've seen examples where specific people were members of 3 or 4 project teams at the same time. In some cases, they are working for 3 or 4 different project managers. Besides trying to keep all the tasks straight, there is a continual challenge for the person to know what is the highest priority task to work on. "Just tell me what to do" is something I hear frequently in this context.

As we have noted, Agile teams are dedicated, stable and focused. The priorities are clear and they are truly able to work on one thing at a time.

Defects

I feel a little sheepish mentioning something as obvious as defects in a list of wastes. I remember my years with traditional projects where we just accepted that there would be defects. We expected them, and built time into the schedule to address them.

What I have learned with Agile teams, is that defects can be dramatically reduced or eliminated entirely. Most of the defects in traditional projects came from poor requirements, sloppy development, or teams working too fast or throwing code 'over the wall'. It really doesn't need to be this way.

Agile teams work to build quality code. They work together with the customer on the analysis and requirements so that they understand what is needed. They use acceptance criteria or specification by example to ensure they are building the right thing. They used test driven development and paired programming to virtually eliminate defects.

Teams over Tasks

Project Management's Dirty Little Secret

Project management's dirty little secret, if it has just one, is that most project managers are control freaks. Yep, you heard it here first. If you are a project manager, either you already knew this or you are in denial. There is no middle ground.

Don't bother sending me your hate mail; I've heard all your arguments before. Control freaks are drawn to project management like moths to a flame. And I think I know why. The attraction to project management is an attraction to tasks and to do lists. Project managers just love to make lists of things to do and then cross things off that list. The best project managers make lists of the various lists!

I know this because I am a pretty good project manager myself. I know what it is like to create lists of lists. I know all about tasks and the sense of success and accomplishment when I cross things off that list.

There is only one small problem, and that is that most people hate to be controlled. Most people don't want to be told what to do; they want autonomy over their work. Autonomy is what gives them a sense of purpose and allows them to thrive. Traditional project managers set up systems that are aligned for conflict.

Parkinson's Law

When I think about my years as a project manager, I think about all the plans, tasks lists, issue lists, risk lists and the like that I created. I loved it! I used to spend hours and hours on my MS Project schedule, getting it just right and trying to get it to match what was actually happening on the project.

Time spent perfecting the project schedule is just one example of project management work that tends to expand to fill the available time. I've been the manager for projects that had only 4 technical resources and large programs that had over 100 resources and in both cases, I was full time. Was it efficient? I don't think so. This is Parkinson's Law at work.

Project Managers are Often Stuck Between a Rock and a Hard Place

I found that as a project manager, I was always trying to balance the capabilities of the team with the expectations of the customer. Often, the customer expectations were set by the promises of someone else, well in advance and were unrealistic. Every hiccup that the team experienced was translated into bad news for the customer. If a team member left the team or made a mistake, or if we collectively missed a deadline, I was the one going back to explain it to the customer.

Sometimes the process worked the other way around as well. Sometimes the customer would demand or request something that just could not be delivered within the plan. It would require extra effort from the team, or would cost additional money. I would be the one who would be explaining this to the team or smoothing over ruffled feathers.

Like many other project managers, I became an expert worrier. (It's also possible I was always an expert worrier looking for a career that needed me!) I worried about every possible scenario and tried to put risk mitigation in place for those. I used to lie awake at night wondering what my team might be forgetting or overlooking.

Agile Teams are Self-Organizing

Things are different with Agile teams. The team is the most important thing – certainly they are more important than the tasks. In fact, thankfully I've not had to use MS Project for several years now.

Rather than needing a project manager to plan their tasks or worry about risks, Agile empowers the teams to do what needs to be done. A couple of principles that relate to this are:

- Principle #5 - Build projects around motivated individuals. Give them the environment and support they need and trust them to get the job done.
- Principle #11 - The best architectures, requirements and designs emerge from self-organizing teams.

To get a sense of what that might look like, here are some characteristics of Agile teams:

- They are co-located, preferably in the same room
- They are cross-functional
- They share knowledge and teach each other
- They are highly collaborative
- They are focused on a small set of activities
- Working together on one item at a time
- They are 7 people +/- 2
- They are full time assigned to team
- They use simple visual management tools

Agile teams don't rely on a project manager to plan for them, to tell them what to do, or to worry about risks. Nor does someone act as an intermediary with the customer. So if you are a project manager in support of an Agile team, you are nearly out of a job. Nearly.

What might an Agile project leader do for an Agile team? Here are my suggestions:

Get the Right People on the Team – We want to build cross-functional teams of motivated individuals. Sometimes we are adding or subtracting based on skills and sometimes it is based on motivation level.

Facilitate, Encourage Collaboration and Teach – An Agile project leader would do well to act more as a coach than as a boss.

Practice Servant Leadership – Servant leaders put the team first. They run interference and remove impediments.

Support Team Growth - Help the team self-organize and move through Tuckman's development stages of forming, storming, norming and performing.

Keep the team together when they are working well – The long term goal is to have stable teams that are high performing.

Last but not least is for the project leader to stay out of the way! The team doesn't need anyone meddling with them or telling them what to do. Project leaders should err on the side of too little involvement, rather than too much.

Adapting over Conforming

Have you ever known a project that was considered a success, even though it may not have been completed on the exact timeframe or budget? Jim Highsmith in his book on Agile Project Management cites the example of the Titanic movie. (Highsmith, 2010)

The Titanic movie won 11 Oscars, and earned over $2.2B, putting it second in terms of highest grossing movies of all time. That same movie cost $200M, which means it earned a staggering 1000% return on investment.

Here's the rub. The Titanic had a budget of $100M, meaning that the project finished 100% over budget. It also went over schedule by 22 days or 16%. Titanic finished shooting in 160 days, which was 22 days over the original schedule of 138. So the project was finished behind schedule, and over budget. According to PM and Standish Group standards, the project is a failure.

A friend of mine has a very successful blog called, "A Girl's Guide to Project Management, Trying to Stay OTOBOS…" OTOBOS stands for On Time, On Budget and On Scope. Is that the right goal for our projects? Should we be conforming to the project plan, or adapting to the conditions that we find? Let's consider some faulty assumptions that traditional project managers may have:

Assumption #1: The plan is the goal

The reality is that achieving the plan is not the goal, delivering customer value is the goal. The Titanic movie planned to cost $100M and it actually cost $200M and it was 22 days over its schedule. Does that mean it was a failure, since it was not delivered on time and on budget? Absolutely not, the film went on to gross $2.2B and earned 11 Oscars. The plan was not the goal; having a great film was the goal.

Assumption #2: That our Plans are Achievable

With traditional projects, we assume that our plans are correct and achievable. We erroneously believe that we can manage our way through complexity and variability. Plan the work, work the plan is our mantra. We often don't consider the possibility that the plans don't make sense or are not achievable.

I like the idea of adapting what we do, rather than trying to conform to our plans. That is the purpose of the Sprint Review and Sprint Retrospective in Scrum, to inspect the product and our process and to learn and adapt. We figure things out as we go.

Assumption #3: That We Need To (or can) Spell Everything Out in Advance

In a traditional project, the customer is concerned about specifying everything up front. They believe that if they don't, they will not get a second chance to specify something that they need. What happens then is an extensive requirements document that has everything but the kitchen sink included. In fact, I've seen these requirements documents that included "critical requirements" that the customer did not even understand, but wanted to include so that they didn't miss anything.

Specifying everything in detail up front can squelch creativity. Worse, there is a real cost of this approach of including everything in the requirements. A recent report from the Standish Group shows that nearly 2/3 of the features and functions in a typical software system are rarely or never used. Imagine the cost involved in that – specifying the requirements, designing the system, developing it, testing and debugging it, documenting it and training on it and deploying it to production.

Chapter 3 Summary

- Agile is a Mindset; a shift in the way we look at work
- Agile is very different from traditional project management

Chapter 4: Agile Overview and Benefits

Key Takeaways for Chapter 4

By the end of Chapter 4, you will be able to:

- Discuss and debunk some common myths about Agile
- Contrast Agile and Traditional project approaches
- Understand some of the most popular Agile methods and frameworks used today
- Look at some of the reasons organizations are adopting Agile, and the benefits they hope to gain

Agile Myths

My experience has been that frequently people have myths and misunderstandings what Agile is all about. Below are some common misunderstandings; we will explore each of these in the sections that follow.

- Agile is a reason to be disorganized or not to plan
- Agile is ad hoc or without processes
- Agile means no documentation
- There are no requirements in Agile
- Agile means no management
- Agile means no discipline

Agile is a reason to be disorganized or not to plan

This particular belief is ironic because Agile teams need to be super organized and are more focused on detailed planning than traditional teams! All Agile team members plan the work together. I've managed large programs with hundreds of team members and never had the level of fine coordination that Agile teams use as they work together on backlog items.

Several years ago when I dove into Agile headfirst, I talked to a friend of mine who was a program manager. When I told him that I was moving into Agile, he said, "Great, who needs a plan?"

Contrary to what you might have heard, Agile teams do plan their work. In fact, this planning tends to be more detailed than the plans done for traditional development. Agile teams use rolling wave planning to plan in detail only the work that is going to be completed in the very near future. And the team members who are going to perform the work are the ones who do the planning.

In his book, *Agile Estimating and Planning*, Mike Cohn describes Agile planning as an onion, with 6 layers as shown below. The three outermost layers of the onion are handled by product management or the PMO, while the inner three layers are the responsibility of the team. We will talk more about planning in Chapter 5 of this book *(Planning Agile Projects)*. For now just be aware that planning for Agile projects is more detailed, comprehensive, and effective than planning for traditional projects.

The Agile Planning Onion

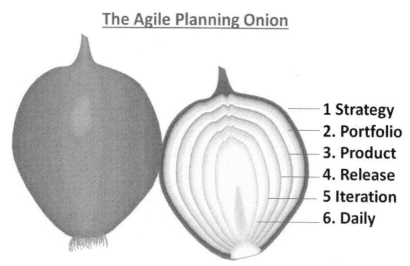

FIGURE 4.1 – THE AGILE PLANNING ONION (COHN, AGILE ESTIMATING AND PLANNING, 2006)

Having planned in both traditional and Agile environments, I would say that there is more planning in Agile teams. Further, the planning is more effective and accurate since it comes as close as possible in time to when the work will be done. This also translates into less waste and more accuracy in planning.

Agile teams work with their business stakeholder, called the Product Owner, to plan a project and break it down into releases. They will work together to breakdown the work into a series of stories and align them to releases. Once they begin to work in iterations, they will plan in detail the work to be done at the start of the iteration. They avoid detailed planning beyond the next iteration to reduce wasted effort. Finally, every day the team will meet to plan their activities for the next day and fine tune their approach.

Agile is ad hoc or without processes

I suspect that this particular myth is based on some early Agile anarchist who didn't want to follow organizational standards and called that lack of process "Agile". The reality is quite the opposite: Agile teams follow a very simple, but highly disciplined set of processes.

As an example, Scrum is a highly disciplined framework which we will explore in the last four Chapters of this book. Scrum prescribes three roles three artifacts. Scrum teams follow a regular sequence of 4 meetings that must occur every iteration without fail. Teams have some flexibility in other things, but not in the framework. Scrum is deceivingly simple to understand, but extremely difficult to exercise with discipline.

Agile means no documentation

Another common Agile myth is that Agile teams do not produce documentation. This is completely false. It is true that one of the Agile values is delivering working software over comprehensive documentation. However, that doesn't mean there is no documentation. Agile teams may produce requirements documents, or create specifications by example (SBE) that represent the functional requirements. Or, the working software and the set of comprehensive automated tests are used in place of system design documentation. But that doesn't mean there is no documentation. Rather, as Alistair Cockburn says, the documentation should be barely sufficient, meaning, just enough. (Cockburn, 2007) It is also just in time.

There are no requirements in Agile

I think this particular myth was invented to scare traditional organizations away from Agile. Many organizations have grown attached to their Business Requirements Documents (BRDs)! The idea of having no requirements would likely be disturbing to anyone who hasn't experienced an Agile project. The process for gathering and documenting requirements is different with Agile projects.

The main purpose that requirements serve in the traditional project is to document the contract, or the agreement between the customer and the team. The customer often thinks of the requirements as an exact and detailed order they are placing for the solution that they need. Once documented, the development team often goes off to develop the solution in isolation. Systems developed in this fashion often result in surprises at the end.

Requirements documents can be very polarizing, with the customer on one side trying to get everything they asked for, and the team on the other trying to guard against scope creep. A change results in both sides negotiating for a win for their side. Remember the Agile Value that says, customer collaboration *over* contract negotiation.

As noted previously, a major challenge with the traditional approach is that requirements are difficult to capture, and they can change as time passes. The larger the system and longer the time to deliver it, the more chance there will be that the requirements will change. Even if we put more effort into understanding and stating the requirements correctly up front, there will always be a disconnect between the true business need and the actual system that is delivered. The effort we invest in up front requirements can actually backfire by preventing us from harnessing change to our competitive advantage.

While you won't have a business requirements document for the entire project, that doesn't necessarily mean no requirements. The Agile approach is for the development team to partner with the business stakeholders and collaborate on business needs. The requirements are not spelled out in detail in advance, rather, the team and business work together to create a high level list of features, then they begin developing them in priority order, one feature at a time.

Teams will usually start with a user story, which is nothing more than a short statement of the business need. Just prior to development of that item, the team has a conversation with the business stakeholders, and they create whatever documentation is needed. This could be a user interface (UI) sketch, a statement of business rules, a short requirements statement, a specification by example, or acceptance criteria. It also could be no documentation beyond the user story, so long as there is a common understanding between the team and the customer.

Using this approach, changes in priority and in requirements are easily accommodated. New needs are added to the list, and priorities can change at any time for work that is "not started". There is also a reduced chance of building unnecessary or unneeded features. Remember the statistic from Chapter 2 that showed that 64% of features built into systems are rarely or never used.

I guess without the context of trust and a track record of delivering something every couple of weeks, this approach would sound risky to some. Once teams and customers begin to deliver small understandable pieces of the solution every couple of weeks, they begin to trust that they don't need a lot of documented requirements.

Agile means no management

This one is a complete myth – Agile does not mean no management. There needs to be some level of management in any group or team, the question is the extent to which the team is self-managing versus having an external manager like a project manager or a functional or line manager.

Most organizations are based on a clear management structure with lines of control. The term command and control is used to describe how typical organizations operate.

Agile teams are intended to be self-organizing, or at least they aspire to be. They might also be called self-managed or self-directed. This means that there is no external agent directing them. In the organizations I've worked with over the years, the level of self-organizations vs. external management has varied widely. Surprisingly, the size of the organization was not a good predictor of the level of self-organization. I worked with a 100 person internet retailer where the Agile teams were directed by project managers who reported to the PMO. And I've worked with a Fortune 100 financial services firm that eliminated most line managers and empowered the Agile teams to make decisions. In the typical Agile team I have supported, there is a mix of team self-management, and organizational management.

Agile means no discipline

Many Agile-curious individuals may be surprised to learn that Agile teams are highly disciplined. A friend of mine related a story to me where he first thought that Agile teams were like skateboarders – young, carefree and undisciplined. There are a prescribed set of meetings, sometimes called ceremonies or rituals, that must be followed. Teams are expected to be organized to deliver working software every sprint. Teams are expected to manage their technical debt, and maintain working systems by tracking the engineering backlog. They meet daily and use highly visible tracking tools to provide fine grain coordination. From the outside, Agile teams will look more like a drill team than a bunch of undisciplined skateboarders. Agile teams that are undisciplined will be quickly revealed.

I can get a pretty good feel for the health of an Agile organization by the discipline they show during their daily meetings. Many organizations call the meeting a standup meeting, but they actually don't stand up. And while the meeting is supposed to be used by the team for fine grained coordination, many times it is turned into a management status reporting meeting. Let me give you a few examples.

I was coaching in one organization where the department manager held a daily standup meeting with his team. He held the meeting in his office, and everyone stood up except him. He went person by person, and essentially interviewed each to get their status for the last day. The meeting would last at least 20-30 minutes and longer if there were problems. Team members tuned out when others were checking in, and it was clear that it was the department manager who was calling all the shots and keeping track of what everyone was doing. Rather than being a tool for team self-organization, it was a tool for micro-management.

Not surprisingly, this same team had another daily 'standup' at the end of the day. This meeting included the Product Owner and other business stakeholders. It lasted anywhere from 45 minutes to an hour every day at 5pm. The developers hated the meeting! I saw that it sucked the life energy out of 16-18 victims every day.

In another organization I was working in, the PMO Director would lead a daily 'Scrum of Scrum' meetings. The attendees of this meeting were the Scrum Masters from each of the Scrum teams. Unfortunately, these Scrum Masters were actually acting as project managers, and during this daily meeting they were just giving status updates to the PMO Director.

Comparing Traditional Projects to Agile Projects

This book is targeted to those unfamiliar with Agile and helping them understand and make the transition to Agile approaches. The following table summarizes some of the key differences between traditional and Agile approaches. Many of these have already been discussed; the remainder will be discussed in later sections of the book.

Traditional Projects	Agile Projects
Changes are costly; Control Processes are used to minimize change	Changes are welcome & expected; Agile Processes embrace change
Business stakeholders are most involved at the beginning and end of the project	Business stakeholders are engaged throughout the project
Needs are stated as requirements	Needs are stated as user stories
Overall solution is built sequentially, in stages using interim deliverables	Overall solution is broken down into small chunks of working software delivered every iteration
Work is handed off from one specialist to another	Teams work together on one item at a time
Project manager juggles the conflicting priorities of cost, schedule and scope to please all stakeholders	Product Owner sets the development priorities & team determines their capacity to deliver those priorities
Project manager drives the work and makes sure everyone is doing their job.	The Product Owner, Project Leader/Scrum Master, and Team collectively drive the work to be done and hold each other accountable.
Predictive – We know how to do this	**Adaptive** – We will learn as we go how to do this.

FIGURE 4.2 - COMPARING TRADITIONAL AND AGILE APPROACHES TO PROJECTS

Quick Agile Quiz

Some of you are in the process of transitioning to Agile, or may have already adopted it. Use this set of 5 questions to do a litmus test of your current organization's agility:

1. Are the Scrum Masters today the former project managers prior to the Agile transition, doing the same activities as before with only a change in title?
2. Is the daily meeting a status meeting, is it facilitated by a manager, or does it takes more than 15 minutes?
3. Do team members operate in silos, rarely collaborating on items, making little effort to learn skills outside their primary skillset?
4. Are the Agile meetings for planning, reviews and retrospectives frequently cancelled or rescheduled?
5. Do functional managers or project managers attend the daily standup to ask questions and provide direction to the team?
6. Are team members required to work overtime or weekends to complete mandated milestones?
7. Do teams make use of large visible information radiators that clearly show their current progress?
8. Do teams self-organize, or does someone outside the team dictate how they work?

Give yourself a point for every yes answer. If you had more than 3 yes responses out of 8, it indicates that there are opportunities to improve your agility.

Popular Agile Methods

VersionOne is a provider of Agile tools, or Application Lifecycle Management (ALM) tools. Every year VersionOne does a survey of Agile users. The most recent survey (2012) included the following table which shows the popularity of various Agile methods. (VersionOne, 2013)

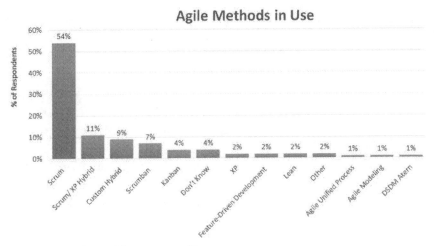

FIGURE 4.3 –AGILE METHODS IN USE

Scrum

As you can see, Scrum tops the list of Agile methods being used at this time, with 72% of respondents indicating that they used Scrum or a Scrum hybrid. That mirrors my own experience. In fact, I've never been involved in an Agile transformation that wasn't Scrum, or Scrum in combination with XP or Kanban. For this reason, we are going to spend all of Chapters 5 through 9 on Scrum. Below is a quick summary:

- Scrum is a framework and not a true methodology. It is often considered a project management approach since it addresses many of the activities that a project manager would handle for a team.

- As mentioned earlier, Jeff Sutherland is credited with developing Scrum along with Ken Schwaber.

- Scrum features timeboxed iterations. Iterations today typically range from 2 to 4 weeks, with 2 weeks being most common. I've heard of teams using 1 week iterations but it requires a lot of discipline. The iteration is really important. Each and every iteration should result in a small subset of the product that is finished and works. That small piece of working software should be **potentially shippable**. This means that all the work necessary to complete that small subset of the product is completed within the iteration, and could be put in the hands of the end user. An interim deliverable like a design document or requirements document does not qualify as potentially shippable. Nor do partially developed features that require testing, or anything else to bring them to a state of being done.

- Scrum is highly disciplined!
- Scrum includes just 3 roles: a Product Owner, Scrum Master and team member. The Product Owner (there is just one) represents the business needs and prioritizes the features to be developed. The Scrum Master is a teacher and facilitator and supports the team by removing impediments and helping the team to self-organize. And the team members, well, they do everything else. That 'everything else' includes analysis, design, development, testing and anything else needed to take a feature or backlog item to completely done. Anyone that is not playing one of these three roles is considered an external stakeholder. Stakeholders may provide subject matter expertise but they are not considered part of the team and they don't make decisions for the team or steer the development.
- Scrum includes 3 artifacts: the Product Backlog, the sprint backlog and a potentially shippable increment. The Product Backlog is a list of all the items needed to be developed to complete the product. The sprint backlog is a subset of the Product Backlog representing the work to be done within the current sprint. And the potentially shippable product increment represents the part of the product that will be completed in the sprint.
- Within the iteration, there is a series of four key meetings. Each meeting has a purpose and a specific set of activities. The daily Scrum is a short meeting used by the team to coordinate their work for the day. The sprint planning meeting is a meeting at the beginning of the sprint, that, like the name implies is used to plan out the sprint. The Sprint Review meeting comes at the end of the iteration, and is used to engage the team, the Product Owner and key stakeholders in a review of the sprint increment. And the Sprint Retrospective is a meeting at the end of the iteration which allows the team to inspect and adapt, by discussing what works well and what needs to be improved.

Extreme Programming (XP)

XP is not a methodology, it is a set of technical or engineering practices that are used to develop solutions. XP has its roots in in the Rapid Application Development approaches that were popular in the 1990s. As mentioned earlier, Kent Beck created XP while working on the Chrysler Comprehensive Compensation (C3) Project at Chrysler.

Many of the technical practices that XP leverages have become common practices even for teams that are not formally adopting XP. Three in particular come to mind. First, continuous integration is the process of integrating new code into the code base on a frequent basis – at least daily and perhaps even hourly or more frequently. The value of this is that all developers are working on the same code base, and integration risks are identified and resolved. The solution is ready to be shipped.

The second common XP practice is pair programming. Pair programming, or pairing, is when you have two developers working together on the same code at the same time. Typically one programmer is driving the keyboard, and the other is observing, questioning, supporting, or learning. While it may seem slower, studies have shown that while paired programming results in a minimal increase in development cost (15%), it results in significant reduction in defects, better code design and fewer lines of code, lowering overall maintenance costs. (Cockburn & Williams , 2000) It also results in productivity gains and intangible benefits like faster problem solving, cross training, and team enjoyment and morale. Since the introduction of XP in 1996, pairing has grown to include more than just pair programming. Pairing can include developers working with testers, analysts working with customers, or any situation where two people are working on the same thing at the same time.

The third common XP practice is automated testing. Automated testing may be a set of Chapter level, functional, or acceptance tests. They are automated in that they either run on a scheduled basis, such as hourly or overnight, or in response to an event, like the check-in of an updated code module. The value of automated tests is that they provide an early indication of problems, and they protect the code base.

Teams may have some form of highly visible signal to indicate failure of the automated tests. Traditionally this was a lava lamp, but teams today may use a red/green screen that is programmed to automatically show the status of the build or test. A red/green screen is either green when all the builds or tests pass, or red when builds or tests are failing. Teams that use automated testing make it a priority to fix the underlying cause of the red screen, so that seeing a red screen is the exception, and not the rule.

Some of the more popular XP practices are described in more detail below. (Beck, 2005)

Whole Team – The point of the Whole Team practice is to have a cross functional team that has all the skills needed to complete the task at hand. The team feels that they are collectively responsible for the results, and they provide mutual support.

Informative Workspace – Alistair Cockburn used the term "information radiator" to describe the big, highly visible tracking tools common in informative workspaces (see diagram at right). Kent Beck said that interested observers should be able to walk into the team space and get a general idea of how the project is going within fifteen seconds. In the picture below, the team has all their tracking charts, task boards, and burndown charts on the walls around them.

FIGURE 4.4 – AN EXAMPLE OF AN INFORMATIVE WORKSPACE

Daily Deployment – Daily deployment (or daily build) is the practice of integrating new code into the code base every day or overnight. Any code that is on a developer's computer that is not in production represents a potential integration issue. While this goal may not be attainable for some teams, it represents a stretch goal that teams should aspire to.

Refactoring – Refactoring is the practice of revising code to improve the design without changing the functionality. Though a key part of XP, refactoring was first introduced by William Griswold and William Opdyke, and popularized by Martin Fowler is his book, *Refactoring: Improving the Design of Existing Code.* (Wikipedia, 2014)

Sustainable Pace – Originally called Energized Work, the intent of this practice is to encourage teams to work only the hours that they can productively sustain over the long haul. While some sources cite 40 hours a week, XP does not have a specific time limit, nor does it ban overtime. Rather, the point is to work at a pace that can be sustained indefinitely.

Shared Code / Collective Code Ownership – Contrary to how code is sometimes owned in rigid silos, shared code implies all the code is owned by everyone, and anyone on the team can improve any part of the system at any time.

On a personal note, one of the teams I was coaching told me that on one of the newer trading platforms, they found that they were changing code that was originally written by the CIO. The CIO was still an active developer and the entire organization practiced collective code ownership.

Planning Game – The planning game is the name of the planning process that occurs every iteration. It involves planning at the release level and at the iteration level. The goal is to "steer the project" into delivery, rather than attempt to predict exact dates. (WikiPedia, 2014)

Small Releases – Just as it sounds, the practice of small releases is to frequently release functionality into production. This helps to gain confidence, reduce risk and provides an opportunity for learning and feedback.

Lean Software Development

Lean software development is a broad category of development tools that has its origins in the lean manufacturing techniques made famous by Toyota. Some of the key concepts of Lean include value stream mapping, elimination of waste and continual improvement.

Mary and Tom Poppendieck are thought leaders in Lean and they have written three different books on the topic. They list the following as the seven principles of Lean Software Development:

1. **Eliminate Waste** – The first step in eliminating waste is to identify anything that does not add value from the customer's perspective. There are seven identified wastes in software development:
   a. Partially Done Work
   b. Extra Features
   c. Relearning
   d. Handoffs
   e. Task Switching
   f. Delays
   g. Defects

2. **Build Quality In** – Rather than inspect for defects (bugs) at the end, teams that build quality in use test driven development to build tests before code is developed. This helps to ensure that all code is written to pass tests.

3. **Create Knowledge** – Knowledge is an organizational asset that is used for competitive advantage. Remember in Chapter 1 where we quoted Toyota product development researcher Dr. Allen Ward saying "Outlearn the Competition". Teams need to make good business decisions on a daily basis, and knowledge is the key.

4. **Defer Commitment** – Teams defer decisions and commitments until the last responsible moment. This is not a way to dodge work or accountability, but rather to be flexible and keep options open.

5. **Deliver Fast** – Delivering things quickly reduces work in progress (and therefore waste) and reduces risk. It also provides a significant competitive advantage.

6. **Respect People** – As noted in Chapter 2, Toyota invested heavily in people and treated them as their most important asset. Toyota strove to 'build people, then build products'. In software development, it is the developers who are the most important asset.

7. **Optimize the Whole** – Optimize the whole means taking into account the entire system when trying to reduce cost or streamline the process. For example, hiring low-cost developers may save money in the short run, but it could also lead to lower productivity, or increases in defects. Value stream mapping is used to analyze the process from the time of the customer order to the collection of payment and to identify ways to shorten the time and reduce the cost. (Poppendieck, 2007)

Kanban

Kanban is considered a subset of Lean Software development and represents a particular way to visualize and improve the flow of work. Kanban (rhymes with bonbon) is a Japanese word that means visual indicator. In a lean manufacturing plant, a Kanban card would be used to indicate that more materials are needed at a particular step in the workflow.

Kanban software development is a card-based signaling system for organizing software development activities which attempts to **maximize throughput** and **minimize work in progress**. Kanban and Scrum are closely related in these goals, though they take different approaches to minimize work in progress.

So how does Kanban work for software development? Teams using Kanban would create a visual management system showing work items as they flow through development. A key feature is to visualize and improve the workflow; make bottlenecks visible.

Kanban is most frequently used with production support or other interrupt-driven environments where arrival rates are not predictable and different items have different priorities and service level requirements.

FIGURE4.5 KANBAN BOARD

An example of such a visual management system, or Kanban Board, is shown in the photo above. With Kanban systems, items flow from left to right. Each column represents a different step in the process (e.g. ready for development, QA, release and out the door). Different rows on the Kanban board represent different levels of urgency (see Fast Lane above). The Kanban board will quickly tell you how many items are in progress and will show bottlenecks in the system.

Another example of a Kanban board is shown below. This one I helped create for a team developing solutions in PeopleSoft. We used the materials we had on hand at the time which was butcher block paper found in the shipping room. As you can see, low tech and low cost materials can create extremely effective visual boards for Kanban teams.

FIGURE 4.6 - A SECOND EXAMPLE OF A KANBAN BOARD

Kanban by itself is simply a method of making the flow of work visible. It doesn't dictate how work gets done. For this reason, Kanban can be used just as effectively with waterfall development teams as it can with Scrum. A common hybrid of Kanban is "Scrumban" which would generally include all the Scrum meetings along with a continuous flow of development. Otherwise, Kanban systems would not make use of iterations, or have reviews or retrospectives.

A couple of key aspects of Kanban are work in progress (WIP) limits and evolutionary process improvements. WIP limits are used to reduce the number of items being worked on at one time in a particular queue. Let's say you have a team of 3 developers and 1 tester working in a Kanban approach with the following 4 queues: ready, development, user testing and done. You may want to set the WIP limits for the development and user testing queues to 6 and 2 to avoid each person having more than 2 items underway at any one time. As testing finishes their work, they pull from development; development does not push items to testing. So, if development had 6 items finished and ready for testing, they cannot pull in a 7th item until testing has taken one or two items. In this way, an inventory or buildup of partially finished items is avoided. What should happen when the testing and development queues are full is that the developer is forced to go over and talk to testing to determine what is going on. They might discover a quality problem, or find that testing just needs some help.

Key Benefits of Agile

What are organizations trying to achieve by going to Agile? I have seen many reasons. For me personally, I think there is a great deal of alignment, focus and transparency which is beneficial. Here are some other top reasons that have been given:

Adapting to change

The ability to quick shift, change direction or pivot is critical to organizations today. Teams and Product Owners can respond to shifting legislation or competitive pressure within one iteration.

Productivity

Agile teams tend to be more focused, and they coordinate their work which helps to make them more productive. And the use of iterations reduces risks of both project overruns and throwaway work. Agile projects also have higher success rates as we will see shortly.

Focus on delivery of customer value early

Extensive and continual customer involvement means more frequent delivery of what customers need.

Respondents to the Version One Annual Survey provided the following responses when asked what were the top 3 benefits of adopting Agile: (VersionOne, 2013)

% of Respondents	Top Benefits Cited By Respondents
90%	Ability to manage changing priorities
85%	Increased productivity
84%	Improved project visibility
84%	Improved team morale
81%	Enhanced software quality
80%	Reduce risk
79%	Faster time-to-market
79%	Better alignment between IT & Business Objectives
76%	Simplify development process
74%	Improved/ increased engineering discipline
74%	Enhanced software maintainability/ extensibility
67%	Manage distributed teams

FIGURE 4.7 - TOP BENEFITS OF ADOPTING AGILE

Standish Group Findings on Agile Projects

In Chapter 1 we talked about the ongoing Standish Group Chaos studies of project success and failure. In 2012, Mike Cohn stated that the Standish group reported that Agile projects success rates were 3X higher than waterfall projects. Correspondingly, failure rates for Agile projects were 1/3 those of waterfall projects. (Cohn, 2012)

Other Studies on Agile Software Value

A comprehensive book on the value of Agile methods comes from David Rico, Hasan Sayani and Saya Sone. In their book *The Business Value of Agile Software Methods: Maximizing ROI with Just-in-time Processes and Documentation*, they look at both the cost and the return on investment of traditional approaches and Agile methodologies. Leveraging data from surveys done by Microsoft, IBM and VersionOne among others, they provide a plethora of data on each method. A subset of the statistics are shown below. (Rico, et al., 2009)

Return on Investment for Agile Methods:

- 31X Extreme Programming (XP)
- 16X Test Driven Development

- 15X Pair Programming
- 5.8X Scrum

In other words, the investment in XP would return 31X, which is incredible!

Additional Benefits – The Human Side

The topic of Agile benefits was discussed at a recent Agile Meetup that I participated in. It was interesting how the Agile practitioners viewed the benefits of Agile methods. The chart below summarizes the findings.

FIGURE 4.8 - BENEFITS OF AGILE

While all of these items are important, I think the last three items on the "more of this column" are extremely important. They reflect the fact that Agile is a very human approach to getting work done. There is a strong sense of community in having a long standing team that you work with and perform well within. Shared learning means that everyone is able to learn from each other, and understand the business or customer better. Finally, Agile should result in teams and customers that are happy, and that sets up a virtuous cycle. Happy teams produce more and are a joy to work with, so customers are happy. Happy customers are a pleasure to work with and inspire the team to produce more. And so on.

Chapter 4 Summary

- Agile is an umbrella term that includes a number of frameworks and methods. Scrum is the most popular of those methods, and is often combined with other methods.

- After Scrum, the three most popular Agile methods include extreme programming (XP) Kanban and Lean Software development. Organizations will frequently use Scrum in combination with one of these other methods.

- A few other methods are used less frequently, these include Feature-Driven Development (FDD), Dynamic Systems Development Method (DSM) and the Unified Process.

- The key benefits of Agile include ability to respond to change, productivity and transparency. Just as important, there are many benefits to the people involved. Agile is a more human way of getting work done.

Chapter 5: Planning Agile Projects

Key Takeaways for Chapter 5

By the end of Chapter 5, you will be able to:

- Compare and contrast traditional and Agile projects and how they are planned
- Look at traditional and Agile project lifecycles
- Review the 6 levels of planning for Agile projects
- Review a simple process for planning an Agile project or release
- Determine people costs for an Agile project

Overview of Planning Agile Projects

This section covers the planning process for Agile projects. We will start by looking at some of the key differences between planning traditional and Agile projects. We will review the project lifecycles for each type of project and how those lifecycles support planning. Then we'll revisit Mike Cohn's planning onion and discuss which parts of the onion are addressed by agile teams. We'll explore a step-by-step process for planning Agile projects at the release level, and then finally we will discuss how to plan the people costs for Agile projects.

Differences between Planning Traditional and Agile Projects

Traditional project planning can be quite elaborate. It often starts with gathering requirements and defining the scope of the project, and results in a baseline project management plan that includes the scope, schedule and budget. The project management plan may also include a quality plan, a human resources plan, a communications plan, a risk plan and a procurement plan. The Guide to the Project Management body of Knowledge describes project planning in the following 20 steps. (Project Management Institute, 2008)

PMI Project Planning Process

1. Develop Project Management Plan
2. Collect Requirements
3. Define Scope
4. Create Work Breakdown Structure
5. Define Activities
6. Sequence Activities
7. Estimate Activity Resources
8. Estimate Activity Durations
9. Develop Schedule
10. Estimate Costs
11. Determine Budget
12. Plan Quality
13. Develop Human Resource Plan
14. Plan Communications
15. Plan Risk Management
16. Identify Risks
17. Perform Qualitative Risk Analysis
18. Perform Quantitative Risk Analysis
19. Plan Risk Responses
20. Plan Procurements

Agile teams will do some or perhaps most of these activities, but rarely would they document them in project management plan the way a traditional team would. Planning documentation would actually be minimal.

Another major difference is in regards to who leads the planning. On a traditional team, the project manager is responsible for the overall planning process. He or she facilitates the estimating process and then generates project budgets and timelines. On an Agile team, there is no one single person responsible for planning. Rather, the whole team is responsible for planning the work, and the team works with the business stakeholders to develop the release plan.

Another difference in planning approaches is the timing of the planning effort. Traditional teams will start the project by creating their project plan document that includes the 20 steps listed above. Agile teams plan the entire project at a high level, but then only plan in detail the work that is in front of them, typically the next iteration. Each iteration is only about 2 weeks long, so the team's plans don't look out farther. This is similar to rolling wave planning, but more extreme. They develop the detail plans just when they are needed, so that there is not wasted effort.

Because the Agile team is planning every two weeks, they get a chance to learn from their experience and improve their processes. In a year, they will plan at least 26 times and perhaps more. Therefore, they are able to learn and fine-tune their approach.

The other key difference between Agile teams and traditional ones is that the Agile plan is not treated as a commitment or a guarantee, at least in most environments. Though not universally accepted, stakeholders in the Agile environment are taught that the Agile team will deliver to the best of their ability, and getting a result different from the plan is not a human performance failure, rather it is either an inaccurate plan or an opportunity to learn and improve. The plan is not a guarantee. This is why it is often called a forecast.

Using Project Lifecycles as Planning Tools

Technology Project Lifecycles

For technology projects, a lifecycle with specific phases may be used to plan out a project. A lifecycle is a model for the life of a project, from beginning to end. The lifecycles I have worked with over the years typically spelled out the steps of the project, the deliverables produced and the resources needed. Take for example the high level project lifecycle shown below. This was the lifecycle used for Oracle projects at a consulting firm where I worked. This approach used 5 different stages, with specific activities going on in each stage.

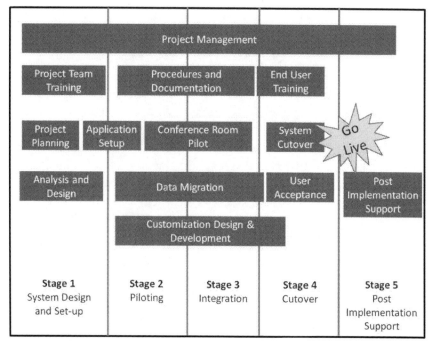

FIGURE 5.1 - A HIGH LEVEL PROJECT LIFECYCLE

At that same company, we used another approach for custom development of ecommerce projects. This approach was definitely influenced by both the Waterfall approach, as well as incremental development. The lifecycle for these custom projects resembled the flow below.

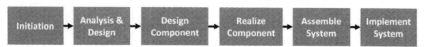

FIGURE 5.2 – LIFECYCLE PHASES FOR A CUSTOM DEVELOPMENT E-COMMERCE PROJECT

Each of the phases listed above spelled out the completion of specific deliverables. Each deliverable was identified, estimated and resources assigned. This drove the project timeline and the budget. Each of the phases listed above was completed sequentially. This was essentially the Waterfall approach we described in Chapter 2.

An Agile Project Lifecycle

As noted above, Agile project lifecycles are different in that they look repetitive and continuous. The following Agile project lifecycle is adapted from Jim Highsmith's *Agile Project Management; Creating Innovative Projects.* Highsmith included 5 phases, with the middle 3 of those being iterative. (Highsmith, 2010).

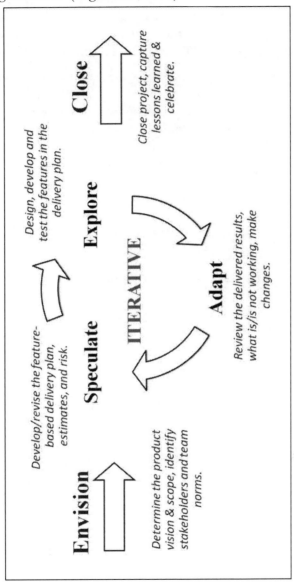

FIGURE 5.3 – AGILE PROJECT LIFECYCLE

A Simplified Lifecycle for Agile Projects

I actually think the Highsmith approach is more complex than it needs to be. In fact, most Agile initiatives might not even be considered a project. We could just stand up an Agile Team and then continue to bring work to them so that they just deliver valuable software without an end. That is a very common approach.

If we do want to treat our initiative as an Agile project, then I recommend a much simpler lifecycle approach than the Highsmith lifecycle; one with just 3 phases. There are a group of activities that need to be done prior to starting to iterate, or "sprint". These can be categorized as "pre-sprint" activities. This would include many of the same upfront or initiation activities that you would do on a traditional project like visioning, business case development, and team formation. It would also include any upfront activities to prepare for development like acquiring equipment, tools and software environments. Some Agile teams use the term "Sprint 0" to identify those preparation activities that are done in advance of the actual sprints.

The next major phase of my simplified lifecycle would include the actual iterations or sprints. This is where the building of the solution takes place in an iterative and incremental fashion. The activities that take place here include all those activities that we described in the previous section. However, they are performed on a very small piece of functionality, and completed within the sprint. Small slices of functionality are developed using all of those activities. The sprinting phase could be viewed as an iterative process starting with analysis and design and repeating as needed.

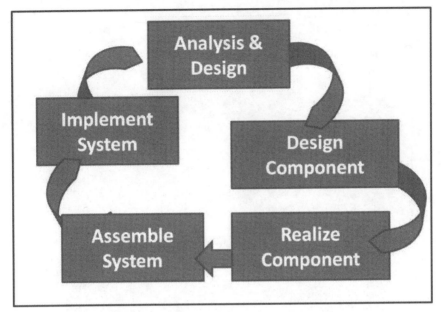

FIGURE 5.4 - THE SPRINTING PHASE

After all the development work is completed in the sprints, the post sprint activities result in solutions being deployed or implemented and the project being closed out. Deployment may include a hardening iteration where final integration and regression testing occurs, though this work should be minimal. Final user testing may take place at this time, as well as any stakeholder communication activities.

This series of three phases is shown in the diagram below.

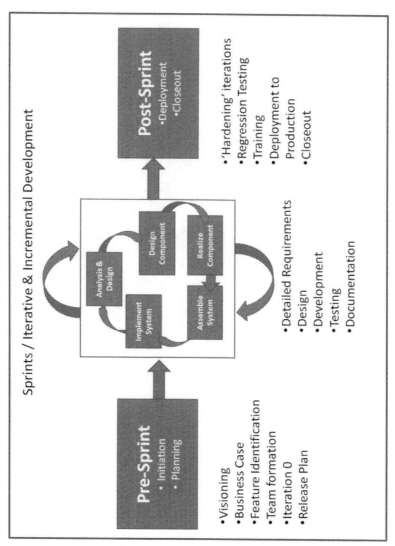

FIGURE 5.5 – A SIMPLE THREE PHASE LIFECYCLE FOR AGILE PROJECTS

In practice, many Agile teams do the first 'pre-sprint' phase once, and then they move into a mode of continuous development and deployment. That continuous mode blends the sprint activity and the post-sprint activities shown above and the teams continue on indefinitely.

Agile Release Planning

In Chapter 4, we introduced the Agile Planning Onion, a concept popularized by Mike Cohn. The first three levels of the onion are typically outside the purview of the agile team. Decisions about organizational strategy and portfolio investments are made by PMOs, business stakeholders, or product management. Agile teams are generally responsible for the last three levels of planning starting with Release Planning. (Cohn, 2006)

The Agile Planning Onion

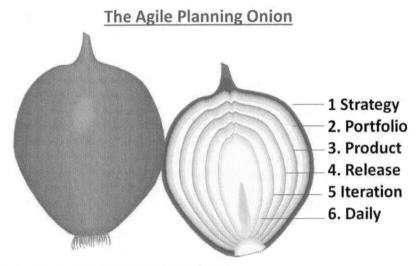

1 Strategy
2. Portfolio
3. Product
4. Release
5 Iteration
6. Daily

FIGURE 5.6 - THE AGILE PLANNING ONION

For Agile teams, release planning is the rough equivalent to traditional project planning. A release is a collection of code which is meaningful to the business or end user. Releases can vary widely and agile teams strive to release frequently with smaller volumes of code. Frequent releases reduce risk.

Release planning helps the team to answer questions that are typical of every project, such as, when it will be done, or how many people we need. It can also be used for what if planning, like when will a specific feature or group of features be complete, or what will be done by a specific date.

Over the years, I've employed a step-by-step process to plan product releases. It's simple and understandable and it is sufficient to get your team started with Agile. I've applied this approach at dozens of companies, with single Agile teams of 3-9 full time people, as well as with larger programs consisting of multiple teams. The process consists of the following 7 steps which are described in the sections that follow.

1. Create a Product Vision
2. Create the Initial Backlog
3. Prioritize that initial Backlog
4. Estimate the Backlog
5. Estimate the Average Team Velocity
6. Create the Release Plan
7. Iterate

(1) Creating a product Vision

The purpose of the product vision is to identify the customers for the product, determine the needs satisfied and outline the value provided by the solution. The vision gets everyone on the team united toward a common goal.

Of all the steps in this simple process, this one can vary the most. Some teams do little or no vision planning, or they leave the vision planning to others. This is common when teams are supporting legacy systems, or supporting systems used by internal teams. On the other hand, teams that are introducing new systems to external users often make the product vision a priority.

There are many tools that can be used to create a product vision. Some teams use the traditional project charter or business case as a vision document. I've worked with teams that used a "four blocker" format to create a one-page vision document. The four sections of the document included the product goal, success criteria, constraints and a high-level milestone plan.

The specific tools or approach are actually less important than the conversations required to create the vision. For that reason, it makes sense to involve the team and relevant stakeholders in the vision process. It would not make sense to have one person go off and create the vision.

Two visioning tools that I recommend for Agile teams are the elevator statement and product box. I've used these extensively. The idea of the elevator statement comes from Geoffrey Moore in his book, *Crossing the Chasm*. (Moore, 1999) Moore proposed a concise, structured way of describing the vision for a product via a statement that answered a series of questions. The idea was that in a short elevator ride with a senior executive, a team member could articulate this short statement to convey what they were working on. The format of the elevator statement is shown below.

For…[description of target customers]

Who are dissatisfied with…[the current alternative to the product]

Our Product is a…[description of new product]

That provides…[key problems being solved]

Unlike…[the product alternative]

We have Assembled…[key product features]

FIGURE 5.7 - THE ELEVATOR STATEMENT FORMAT

I've used the elevator statement exercise many times and find the discussions extremely helpful. The discussion reveals false assumptions, differences of opinions and lack of clarity.

To generate the elevator statement, I will generally assemble the team, the business sponsor or product manager and other stakeholders as appropriate. Using a flip chart, we add the headings on the left, and then we begin to flesh out the statements. The process can be messy and sometimes there are strikethroughs and additions. Once completed, teams will hang the elevator statement in their shared team space. (See example at right.)

You could certainly use a laptop and projector, though I prefer the flipchart. Not only does it constrain the scope of the exercise, it tends to be much more engaging than one person driving a laptop while others read email or do other work. See below for an example of an elevator statement created by a team.

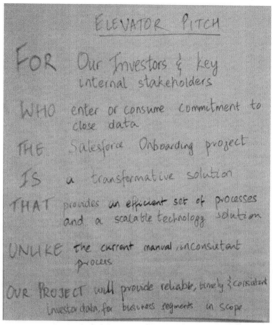

FIGURE 5.8 - AN ELEVATOR PITCH EXAMPLE

As an aside, I once coached Agile teams at a private equity firm where the 3 founding partners often rode the elevator with other employees. One of the partners made a habit of challenging any employees he didn't recognize by asking, "Who are you and what do you do for me?" I was coached to tell them my name and say that I "worked for the investors", though unfortunately I never had a chance to use it.

The second visioning approach that I like to use with Agile teams is the product box. This approach is described in *Innovation Games* by Luke Hohmann. (Hohmann, 2007) With the product box, the team works together to create a box that would represent the product if it were on the shelf in a store. Teams have to think about what would be on the box, what color the box would be, etc.

The process of creating the box can be very lively. Some teams create a physical box; others will draw a representation of the front and back of the box on pieces of flip chart paper. As a facilitator, I like to offer colored markers, stickers, colored papers and other materials to encourage creativity. Teams are encouraged to list out the key benefits on the front, draw pictures or create graphics to represent the product and list out key system requirements on the back of the box. A couple example product boxes drawn on flip charts are shown below.

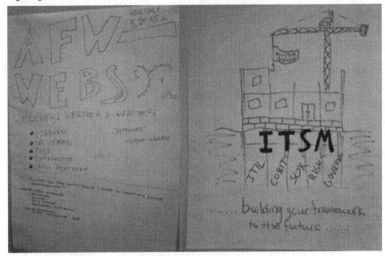

FIGURE 5.9 - EXAMPLES OF PRODUCT BOXES

(2) Create the Initial Backlog

After defining the product vision, the next step is to create an initial backlog. The backlog is the list of all the features and functions that need to be built. The backlog is not a work breakdown structure or a task list, it is written at the feature and function level. As an example, compare the feature breakdown for creating a video on the left below, to the task breakdown on the right.

Feature Breakdown	Task Breakdown
Introduction video	Create story board
Key Benefit #1 video	Create script
Key Benefit #2 video	Identify actors
Key Benefit #3 video	Shoot scenes
Summary video	Edit scenes
	Edit final video

FIGURE 5.10 - INITIAL BACKLOG

Teams often begin by identifying the major functionality to be delivered as part of the system. This effort is generally led by the business sponsor, or in Scrum, the Product Owner. The team works together with the sponsor to break the release down into specific features, or user stories. This is usually a top down process with large chunks of functionality being identified which are later broken down into individual features or backlog items.

Those individual features or backlog items are commonly called user stories, based on the concept of stories which originated in XP. A user story is a description of how a user will use a system to accomplish some goal. We will look at the specific format of the user story when we talk about the Product Backlog in Chapter 9.

Extending the "story" analogy, many Agile teams use the term "Epic" to refer to a large story or feature group that is not yet broken down into smaller pieces. You may find this term used inconsistently on Agile projects and in particular in the way it is implemented in tools that support Agile teams. Some teams use Epic to mean a really big story, and others use it to mean a category of user stories.

The process of starting with the Product Vision, and breaking that down into epics and stories is called progressive elaboration. This is shown in the graphic below.

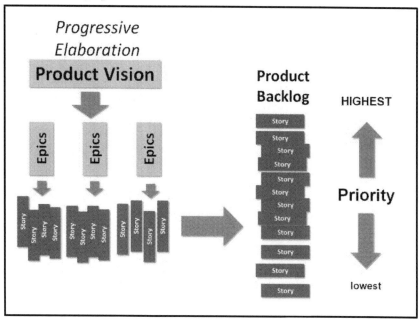

FIGURE 5.11 - THE PROGRESSIVE ELABORATION OF EPICS AND STORIES

Over time, each user story gets broken down into small enough items or stories that they can be delivered within one iteration or sprint. A helpful rule of thumb from Craig Larman is that an item should take up no more than 1/3 of an iteration. Smaller than this is fine and sometimes unavoidable, but larger items should be broken down or split.

The initial backlog is just a starting point – we fully expect that it will change over time. For this reason, we don't expend too much effort trying to get it exactly right, or to get a customer signoff that the backlog is complete. It isn't complete, and a signoff would be meaningless. New items will be discovered as we begin work and learn more, and the team should expect that the backlog will change.

(3) Prioritize the Backlog

Once the initial backlog is created, it needs to be prioritized so that the team works on the most important features first (see graphic above). Prioritization is led by the business sponsor. The highest priority items are usually those that provide the most business value.

Though led by the business sponsor, the team supports the prioritization and can make priority recommendations based on technical dependencies and risk. Items that are technically risky are usually moved higher in the backlog, so that risk is not deferred to the end of the project.

Unlike a requirements document where we might have assigned High, Medium and Low priorities to each requirement, the Product Backlog is rank-ordered based on priority. That means that the project backlog is prioritized from top to bottom, with the most important items at the top. If you have ever been in discussions with stakeholders and heard that every requirement is critical, you will appreciate having a list of items that is prioritized from most important to least.

Just as with adding new items to the backlog, we should also expect that the priorities can change at any time. It is up to the business sponsor to change the priorities.

(4) Estimate the Backlog

Once all the features or stories are identified, broken down and prioritized, the team estimates each of the items that will be included in the release being planned. Teams will use a process called relative estimation at this point to get fast estimates without a lot of information. Relative estimates means that the items are compared to each other and not to some absolute measure. Relative estimation is not highly accurate, but it is accurate enough.

T-Shirt sizes and story points are common relative estimating units. T-shirt sizes are the sizes you would find for t-shirts in a store, from extra small (XS) through to extra-large (XL) or even XXL.

Story points follow the Fibonacci series (or Cohn series). Teams generally use story point estimates based on the scale shown below in figure 5.12. Items that are bigger than 21 are broken down so that they fit the scale.

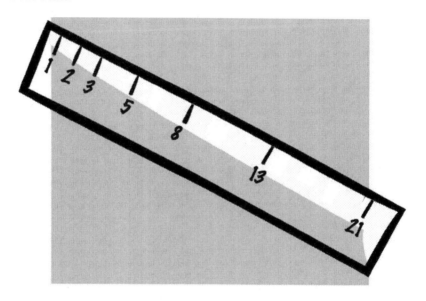

FIGURE 5.12 - A COMMON SCALE FOR ESTIMATING STORIES

So how do you determine the size of a story? Teams will usually select a story or two that are well understood in order to do relative estimating. It is best to have a small and a large story to serve as reference stories as a basis for estimating. Set the small story somewhat arbitrarily to 2, and the large one to 8 or 13. Then, based on those two stories, estimate everything else in the backlog. This provides a fast estimate.

One specific approach to relative estimating is called planning poker. With planning poker, the team reviews a particular backlog item, and then each team member determines their estimate without revealing that to the others so as to avoid bias. When everyone has their estimate prepared, the team all reveals their estimate at the same time. If everyone had the same estimate, that becomes the team's estimate for the item. More frequently, the team differs on the estimate. In that case, the team discusses the high and low outliers, explores the rationale for the differences and then re-votes.

In addition to being fast, a key benefit of planning poker is the discussion that ensues. The discussion reveals assumptions and helps share the knowledge within the team. I believe that the discussion is more valuable than the actual estimate that is produced!

As noted in Chapter 2, planning poker was created by James Grenning. Mike Cohn popularized the term in his book Agile Estimating and Planning and has trade marked the term. The origins of planning poker are the Wideband Delphi estimating technique which was created by the RAND Corporation in the 1950's. (Wikipedia, 2014)

Another approach to estimating a lot of stories is to do affinity estimating. Using this approach, teams quickly separate stories into piles based on either story point size, or T-Shirt size. A team can divide and conquer and sort the piles quickly. I usually establish a pile labeled as "?" for items that need to be discussed. The team spends more time on these items than the ones that do not require discussion. In this case, the team estimated about 50 stories in just under an hour. Once the team sorted all the stories into the sizes shown, they converted those T-shirt sizes to story point estimates.

(5) Estimate the Team Velocity

The next step in release planning involves making a guess of the team velocity. Velocity is a measure of the throughput of the team, or how fast the team converts backlog items into valuable software. Velocity is measured on a per iteration basis. A team that can complete 34 story points per iteration would have a velocity of 34.

Existing teams will have established an average velocity that can be used as a predictor of the future. Usually the average of the previous 3 sprints is used as the estimate for future sprints. Teams may also use best and worst averages for best and worst case forecasts.

For new teams, a guess will need to be made for the velocity. One approach is to identify a few stories from the backlog that the team thinks they can complete in an iteration and use that as an initial velocity. It sounds a little imprecise, and it is. However, it is precise enough to get things started and once teams complete an iteration they can use their actual velocity. New teams will usually see their velocity increase and then stabilize after 4-6 iterations.

(6) Create the Release Plan

Once the team knows the backlog size and the velocity, they can estimate the release. The basic math is Backlog Size / Velocity = Number of Iterations. We use the velocity to allocate stories to iterations or sprints. When all the stories needed for the release are included, we draw the line in the backlog for the release as shown in the diagram below.

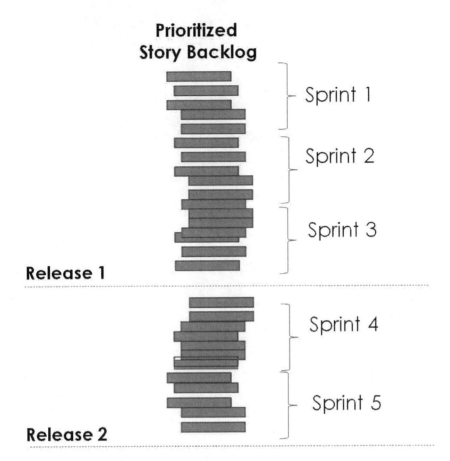

FIGURE 5.13 - PRIORITIZED STORY BACKLOG

A release may need to include some empty iterations for planning purposes. These are called buffer sprints, and they provide some room in the schedule for unanticipated work. Hardening sprints are similar, though hardening sprints are used to complete testing, training, or any other work that needs to be done, outside of new functionality. In an ideal world, teams would complete everything within the sprint and there would be no need for hardening sprints. Unfortunately, this is often not the case and hardening sprints need to be added to provide realistic release date estimates to stakeholder.

The chart below shows two different options that are available to create the release plans. The option described on the left side of the chart is for scope driven dates. With scope driven dates, the release date is flexible, based on all the stories that must be completed in the release. The chart shows a buildup of user stories completed as well as those stories remaining to be completed. The dashed line shows the forecast for completion and is being used to predict the release date.

Another option is shown on the right – date driven scope. With this approach, the release date is fixed and the contents of the release are allowed to flex. The amount of the scope that can be completed is estimated based on the average velocity, and slower and faster velocities.

Option 1: Scope Driven Date
(We won't release until we get all the critical features).

Option 2: Date Driven Scope
(Date and Velocity determine what will be released)

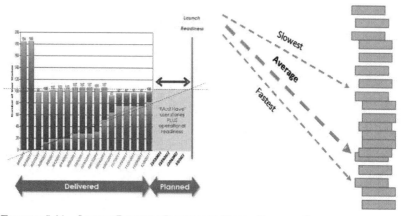

FIGURE 5.14 – SCOPE DRIVEN DATE AND DATE DRIVEN SCOPE

Tracking to release plans need not be complicated. The simple chart shown below hung in the team area for a team developing Salesforce.com solutions. The horizontal dashed line shows that they needed 177 story points for their go-live on 3/31. The shaded bars showed progress toward that goal.

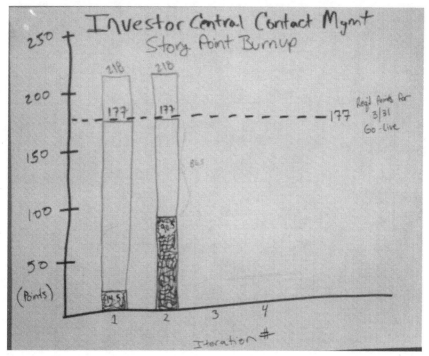

FIGURE 5.15 – SAMPLE RELEASE PLAN TRACKING

(7) Iterate the Plan

Once you create the initial release plan, are you done? Absolutely not! Velocity tends to vary and may be a guess. Stories may be added or deleted from the scope of the release as we complete work and learn. Teams need to review where they are and how fast they are progressing and then update their release plans accordingly. I recommend that the release plan be reviewed and updated at the end of each iteration.

You might also revisit the plan more frequently if there are significant changes to the backlog or the composition of the team. Any change to the team composition will usually lead to an initial drop in velocity.

I once worked with a team that was delivering a custom solution to an external client. The client had a prioritized Product Backlog that represented all the functionality they thought they needed. However, they wanted to complete the work as early as possible. So, the client was diligent about carefully evaluating the solution being delivered and whether the remaining stories in the backlog were needed or not. As delivery progressed, the client was able to eliminate future stories and reduced their story points in the backlog from 435 to 375. This allowed them to cut a full month of development and release from the plan. The charts below show the release plan after the end of the 8th iteration, and then the revised release plan after the end of the 11 iteration below.

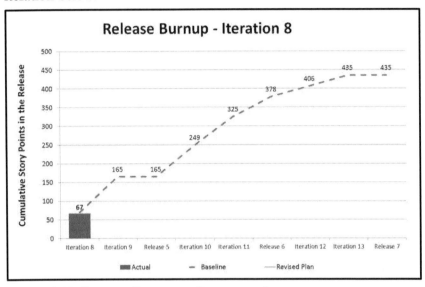

FIGURE 5.16 - RELEASE BURNUP AT ITERATION 8

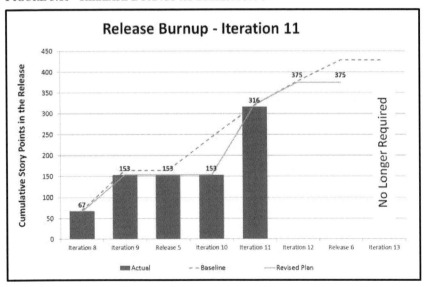

FIGURE 5.16 - RELEASE BURNUP AT ITERATION 11

The seven step process described above works at the team level and can be scaled up on a team by team basis.

The remaining two levels of planning from Mike Cohn's planning onion are iteration planning and daily planning. We will discuss these in detail in Chapter 8.

Budgeting for People Costs on Agile Projects

Traditional Staffing Levels through the Project lifecycle

Those familiar with the Project Management Body of Knowledge (PMBOK® Guide), will recognize the diagram below showing staffing levels over the life of a project. In general, project staffing levels start out low as initial planning work gets underway, peak when the project is being executed and diminish as the project is closed. (Project Management Institute, 2008)

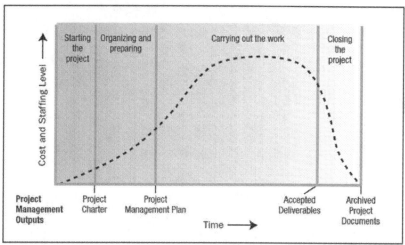

FIGURE 5.18 - TYPICAL COST AND STAFFING LEVELS ACROSS A PROJECT

Staffing Levels for Agile Projects

Planning for people costs on Agile projects is relatively straightforward. Rather than use deliverables and tasks to determine people costs, we treat teams as stable, at least for a project, and we plan costs at the team level. We use the timeline from the release plan, determine the average people costs per sprint, and use those two inputs to calculate people costs over the life of the project.

This is only possible by using stable teams, which may seem hard for traditional managers to appreciate. One of the goals of Agile is to create long term stable teams that have cross functional skills. These stable teams work closely together for long periods of time and strive to maximize productivity. They are not treated as individuals; they work together in a team. Each team has from 5 to 9 team members and we avoid adding or removing team members. The first decision to be made when planning an Agile project would be, how many cross functional teams are needed.

If this is the first Agile project in the organization, it might help to think about the skills needed and the specific people that would typically be assigned to a project like this. Converting the resource levels of a comparable plan to full time equivalents (FTEs) will tell you roughly how many resources are needed. Divide this by 7 to get a rough idea of number of teams.

If you have an existing project that is underway, it might be easier to plan a transition to using Agile. Assuming you have a mix of full time and some part time people on the team, you simply convert the number of people to FTEs and then use that as a guideline for the number of cross-functional teams. For Agile teams, you will want to have all full time, dedicated resources. So if you would have used 5 full time people and 7 shared people on the team, you would probably want to select 7 or 8 people to be on a full time team. You may have to do some cross training to address skill or knowledge gaps, and you will probably have to do some negotiating to get all full time resources – no one said it would be easy!

Several years ago I was helping to transition a large program to Agile. We went from one large program team to 11 separate, cross-functional teams. We staggered the transition to Agile over 5 months, to reduce chaos. The chart below shows the timeline for the transition of each team from traditional development to Agile.

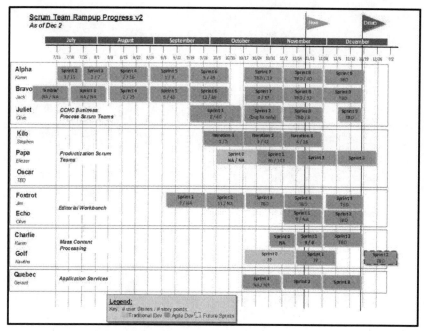

FIGURE 5.19 – PROGRAM TRANSITION TO AGILE

If we look at the people on Scrum teams, the corresponding staffing chart for this program startup might look something like the one below. Eventually, all the teams were initiated and then the staffing levels looked like a flat line.

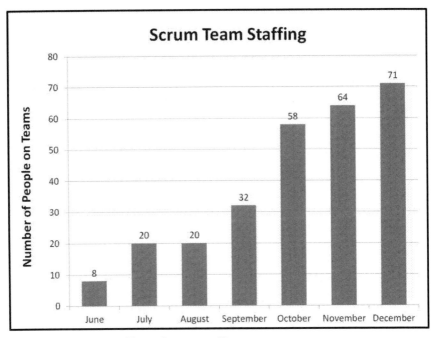

FIGURE 5.20 - SCRUM TEAM STAFFING EXAMPLE

Budgets for Agile Teams

Once the staffing levels are determined, budgets are straightforward to calculate. Simply determine the monthly run rate based on the number of people on the team.

Organizations that have created long-term stable teams have an even easier time. Long term stable teams have the same team members. Costs are very simple and predictable.

Chapter 5 Summary

- Unlike traditional projects, Agile projects do not have a lifecycle that can be used to drive planning. Instead, plans are based on backlog size and team velocity.

- Agile planning includes 6 different levels, with teams focusing on release, iteration and daily planning.

- Release planning starts with product vision and results in a timeline for completing the functionality included in the release.

- Planning for agile resources is done based on full time participation on teams that are stable.

Chapter 6: An Introduction to Scrum

In chapter 2, we talked briefly about Scrum, the most popular Agile project management framework being used today. The remainder of this book will focus on the ins and outs of Scrum. We will look in detail at how Scrum works, and the roles, meetings and artifacts used in Scrum. You will come away with a good understanding of Scrum and how it is used for organizational change.

Key Takeaways for Chapter 6

By the end of Chapter 6, you will be able to:

- Provide an overview of Scrum, the 3 Scrum Principles and the 5 shared values
- Introduce the Scrum roles, artifacts and meetings
- Discuss that though Scrum is a simple framework, it can be a very powerful tool for organizational change
- Learn that Scrum is based on the principles of Transparency, Inspection and Adaptation
- Understand a Scrum diagram that we will use for the remainder of the book

Scrum Overview

You have to admit, Scrum is a pretty unlikely sounding word for a product development framework. As described in Chapter 1, the term actually came from the game of Rugby, where the Scrum (short for scrimmage) is a way of restarting play where both teams line up opposing each other with all players interlocked. During the restart, each team is single-mindedly focused on taking possession of the ball and moving it downfield.

Authors Takeuchi and Nonaka saw this same principle of single-minded focus applied in highly effective product development teams. They called this the Rugby approach, in contrast to the traditional sequential process that they called the relay race approach. (Takeuchi, 1986)

Jeff Sutherland built on the idea of the Rugby approach, and called his process Scrum. Scrum teams use the concept of moving the ball downfield by focusing their collective efforts on the same mission. Scrum teams use short iterations called sprints – usually from one to four weeks long - to create a steady rhythm of delivery. During each sprint, teams work to complete one item at a time, in priority order.

It is important to note that Scrum is not just for software development. I've seen it applied in different non-technical settings such as business process improvement and even with a sales team. Jeff Sutherland coached venture capital firm OpenView Venture Partners to use Scrum to run their investment practice. (Sutherland, 2 Apr 2012)

Empirical Process Control

Scrum is a powerful tool for empirical process control which is useful for complex adaptive systems like developing new products in an organization.

"The empirical model of process control provides and exercises control through frequent inspection and adaptation for processes that are imperfectly defined and generate unpredictable and unrepeatable outputs."
(Wikipedia, 2012)

Here is a description of complex adaptive systems from Doug DeCarlo that I have found helpful:

Living systems such as projects are complex in that they consist of a great many autonomous agents interacting with each other in many ways. The interaction of individual agents is governed by simple, localized rules and characterized by constant feedback. Collective behavior is characterized by an overlaying order, self-organization, and a collective intelligence so unified *that the group cannot be described as merely the sum of its parts. Complex order, known as <u>emergent order</u>, arises from the system itself, rather than from an external dominating force. These self-organizing Complex Adaptive Systems (CAS) are <u>adaptive</u> in that they react differently under different circumstances and <u>co-evolve</u> with their environment. (DeCarlo, 2004)*

A complex adaptive system is one which cannot be planned or controlled. Instead, the agents of the system self-organize and interact in apparently random ways. A beehive is an example of a complex adaptive system. There is no overall governing plan for the hive; each bee acts according to a few simple rules of behavior and the hive emerges as a result.

With complex adaptive systems, the inputs and the actions of all the independent actors cannot be controlled. Scrum provides a framework to inspect the results of the process, and then adapt the process. Inspection and adaptation are two of the key principles of Scrum as we will see below.

The Scrum Framework

Scrum is a pretty simple framework, consisting of 3 Scrum principles, 5 Scrum values, 3 roles, 3 artifacts and 4 meetings. (Sutherland & Schwaber, 2011) That is all there is to it. We will explore each of these in the sections that follow.

Scrum Principles

The three Scrum principles are often described as the three legs of a stool. These are the tools needed to support empirical process control. Empirical process control is used in complex adaptive systems as a tool to adjust our approach based on the results we are getting.

FIGURE 6.1: THE 3 SCRUM PRINCIPLES

Transparency – We make everything we do visible. Nothing is secret or hidden.

Inspect – We examine the results we get.

Adapt – We adapt our approach based on the results we got.

Scrum Values

Scrum is based on the following 5 shared values – each is described in more detail below:

- Commitment
- Focus
- Openness
- Respect
- Courage

Commitment – Scrum teams must be willing to commit to a goal. Scrum provides people all the authority they need to meet their commitments.

Focus – Focus is about doing your job without distractions. Scrum teams are supported to focus all their efforts and skills on the work that the team has committed to do. They shouldn't be distracted with anything else.

Openness - Scrum advocates that team members are open about how they are doing, about any impediments or concerns so that they can get help if needed.

Respect - Individuals are shaped by their background and their experiences. It is important to respect the different people who comprise a Scrum team.

Courage – Scrum teams are encouraged and supported to act with courage in all that they do. Teams need to know that they will be supported to show courage.

Scrum at a Glance

The diagram below shows the roles, artifacts and meetings of Scrum. Let's walk through the diagram and understand what it is trying to tell us.

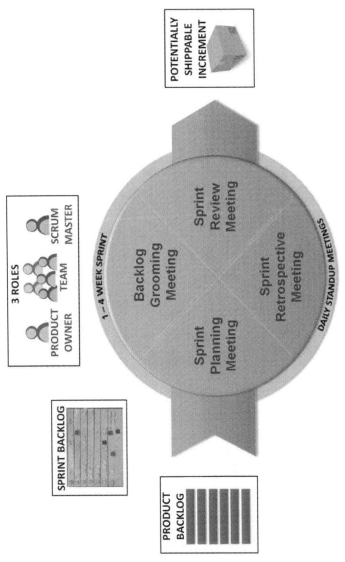

FIGURE 6.3 - ROLES, ARTIFACTS, AND MEETINGS OF SCRUM

3 Roles of Scrum

The diagram below highlights the 3 roles of Scrum. They are, the Product Owner, the Scrum Master and the Team. Everyone has one of these 3 roles, or they are outside Scrum and perhaps just considered a stakeholder.

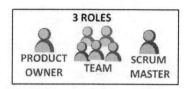

FIGURE 6.4 - THE THREE SCRUM ROLES

There is just one Product Owner in Scrum for each team, and it is their job to prioritize the backlog and make decisions. The Product Owner steers the development by selecting which backlog items are worked on first.

There is just one Scrum Master per team as well, and it is their job to help the team to self-organize and master Scrum. The Scrum Master also removes impediments from the team so that they can be productive.

And then there is the team itself. The team is sometimes called the Development team or the Feature team. The team is comprised of 5 to 9 people, with cross functional skills.

Scrum Meetings

The diagram below lists the 5 Scrum meetings or ceremonies. They are the Daily Scrum, Sprint Planning, Backlog Grooming, Sprint Review and Sprint Retrospective. A 5th meeting that is not formally part of Scrum, called Product Backlog Refinement, is usually needed and included in the Scrum framework. This meeting may also be called backlog grooming.

FIGURE 6.5 - THE SCRUM MEETINGS

Each of the meetings has a purpose, a structure and a timebox that is proportional to the length of the sprint in most cases. They are intended to be focused and productive.

3 Scrum Artifacts

Finally, there are 3 artifacts that support Scrum. The artifacts are the Product Backlog, the Sprint Backlog and the Potentially Shippable Product Increment (PSPI). The Product Backlog represents all the known work that needs to be done to produce the product. The Sprint Backlog is the list of backlog items and tasks that need to be done within the current iteration. And the Potentially Shippable Product Increment is the result of the sprint, the working software.

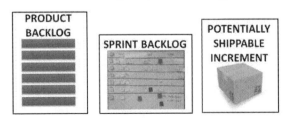

FIGURE 6.5 - THE THREE SCRUM ARTIFACTS

Easy to Understand, Difficult to Apply

Scrum is a very simple framework and most people find it very easy to understand. The Scrum Guide is the definitive explanation of Scrum and it is just 16 pages long. (Sutherland & Schwaber, 2011) Don't be fooled. This very simple framework may be easy to understand but it is extremely powerful, and it can be very difficult to apply.

One thing that makes Scrum hard to apply is the amount of discipline it requires. In fact, it is one of the most disciplined frameworks I have ever used. Once teams agree to a length for their sprint, they need to stick to it and not change from sprint to sprint. If something doesn't get completely done in a sprint, it is not done and the team gets no credit for the partial work they did. No one outside the team is allowed to speak at the daily Scrum or standup meeting. No one outside the team can introduce new work into the sprint once it is started. These are just some of the examples of discipline required.

One thing that I failed to appreciate early in my Agile experience was that Scrum is more than just a software development framework for teams, it is a tool for cultural change. Craig Larman is adamant that Scrum is a force for organizational change, rather than a methodology.

"...in a larger product group (say, 500 people) adopting large-scale Scrum, systemic weaknesses are exposed in the organizational design – in structure, processes, rewards, people, and tasks. In this case, large-scale Scrum is a force for organizational change. This dynamic reflects the lean metaphor of lowering the water level – Scrum is a framework for making the rocks visible. Lowering the water is easy, the hard part is removing the rocks – especially when they involve organizational policy and structure."

(Larman & Vodde, 2009)

Scrum serves as a tool to make organizational weaknesses and impediments visible, like lowering the water level in the pond to make the rocks visible. Scrum is hard not so much because of lowering the water, but because seeing the rocks is difficult. Some examples of rocks or organizational weaknesses are shown in the diagram below.

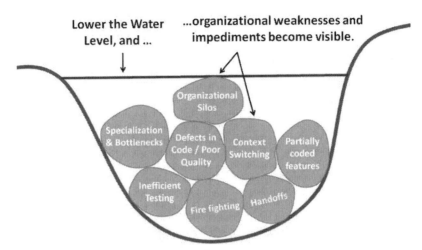

FIGURE 6.6 - SCRUM IS A FORCE FOR CHANGE

Here are some ways that Scrum serves to lower the water level in an organization

#1 - Short cycles (e.g. 2-week sprints) – Scrum teams use short iterations or sprints, during which they take their backlog items all the way from "not started" to "done". These short cycles allow the team to see more clearly the bottlenecks, constraints and difficulties in the system.

#2 - Lower work in progress (WIP) – Scrum teams work on only a small number of items at the same time during an iteration. Like the short cycles, this focus on just a few items reveals impediments and bottlenecks. Teams are able to see and challenge things that slow them down. Queues, delays and specialization become visible.

#3 – Definition of Done – A clear definition of done forces teams to consider all the steps necessary to make a backlog item done or potentially shippable. The definition of done incorporates all organization requirements or standards, and it applies to all the backlog items. Unlike acceptance criteria for one story, the definition of done is not specific.

A definition of done for a team I recently coached includes the following:

1. Requirements documented
2. Designed
3. Developed
4. Tested
5. Refactored
6. Documentation completed
7. Acceptance Tested

Any differences between the definition of done for a sprint, and definition of done for a release is work that needs to be done later, or undone work. This frequently includes regression testing, integration, training and sometimes documentation.

The difference between the definition of done for a sprint and definition of done for a release represents organizational weakness. Optimally, teams could release all their code at the end of a sprint.

As an example, consider a large financial services organization I coached for a year. There were many organizational impediments. The impediments included somewhat innocuous ones like the rigid floor plan layout that didn't support team spaces, the ban on all types of cameras including webcams, an onerous and paperwork-laden release process, or the distribution of teams and Product Owners across 8 locations and 5 time zones.

Then there were the other, more difficult and usually deeply ingrained impediments. These included the annual performance review process which pitted individuals against their teammates by focusing on individual accomplishments. There was a top-down, command and control culture which stifled individual initiatives and fostered dependency on managers. The organization was aligned by application silos, where there were commonly handoffs between teams and a lack of big picture thinking. There were areas of the business that were supporting regulatory reporting which was chaotic and overwhelming, causing burnout and high turnover. Finally, there was significant accumulation of technical debt due to a legacy code base that was difficult to understand and costly to maintain.

Part of the challenge of the organizational impediments is that once you are in the environment for a while, you either lose sight of these types of problems, or you begin to accept them as "just the way things are around here". You lose your objectivity and you continue to work around the difficulties and impediments in the organization. And it comes at the cost of reduced productivity.

As a tool for culture and organizational change, Scrum makes those weaknesses visible, but it doesn't prescribe how to fix the problems. Once you set up Scrum teams and begin operating with a continuous improvement mindset, you begin to bump into these big "rocks". Rather than saying that Scrum doesn't work in your environment, you use it as a tool to begin to make changes. With courage, you can begin to tackle them and "fix the organization" as Craig Larman describes it.

Consider the simple example of the camera ban mentioned above. This example came from a financial services organization and the ban on cameras applied to the trading floor. The ban did not extend to the floor where the technology teams worked. However, due to a misclassification, cameras were banned on all floors of this particular building, including the team areas. It took a lot of work to find the correct person within the organization to change the floor classification.

Is Scrum the Agile Gateway Drug?

In some respects, Scrum could be considered the Agile gateway drug. Teams often start with Scrum and then expand into using other Agile approaches like Kanban or XP. After all, the goal of the organization is not to adopt Scrum, right? The goal of the organization should be to use tools that allow for the evolution of a lean organization that maximizes throughput, and instills a continuous improvement mindset to remove inefficiencies and impediments. Scrum is not the end; it is a means to an end. The goal is continuous improvement, not great Scrum. So it is not a surprise when teams start with Scrum and then evolve into other agile methods.

I do become concerned when agile teams strive to adopt Scrum, or any other Agile method, and they feel that they need to customize it right out of the blocks. Without looking at their big rocks, they decide that Scrum won't work or needs to be tailored.

Other organizations try Scrum or some other agile approach and then immediately decide it is not going to work. They shouldn't. They should try the Scrum framework as it is designed, and then only after getting some experience, they should feel free to change it.

Alistair Cockburn introduced a Japanese martial arts concept "Shu Ha Ri" to teams learning Agile, and I have found this helpful. The idea is that beginners will go through three levels of practice as they learn and master something. The first level is Shu, where as a student you simply do everything exactly as the instructor says. You follow all the rules. You internalize the rules and process by repetition, doing this over and over. The student is not thinking; they are simply following the rules as they have been taught. (Cockburn, 2007)

In the second level, Ha, the student begins to break the rules. By breaking the rules, the student begins to understand exceptions to the rules, or situations where it is advantageous to not follow the rules.

In the third and final level, called Ri, the student leaves the rules behind. The student transcends the rules, and begins to make up their own rules.

This same learning and mastery process can be applied to Scrum. As you begin to apply it, you evolve, and eventually you can make your own rules. Just make sure that your evolution from Scrum isn't just your way of making things up as you go or avoiding the tough work of changing the organization.

I like to ask teams that are quick to change Scrum, what is it you are evolving toward? What is the ultimate goal? How are you measuring it?

What's Next?

In the next few units, we are going to dive into more detail on some areas of Scrum that were introduced in this unit. Chapter 7 will focus on the roles and rules of Scrum. Chapter 8 will focus on the Scrum meetings. And chapter 9 will focus on the Scrum artifacts. Finally, in chapter 10 we will spend some time going through a day in the life of the Scrum team.

Chapter 6 Summary

- Scrum is a simple framework that is easy to understand, but difficult to apply and do well.
- Scrum is a tool for organizational improvement. By applying Scrum, organizational impediments and weaknesses are revealed and can be tackled.

Chapter 7: The Roles and Rules of Scrum

Remember that we said that Scrum is simple. Scrum consists of just three roles: the Product Owner, the Scrum Master and the team. And there are surprisingly few rules. In this Chapter we will explore each of these in some detail.

Key Takeaways for Chapter 7

By the end of Chapter 7, you will be able to:

- Explain in detail the Scrum roles, including Product Owner, Scrum Master and team
- Understand the importance of self-organizing teams
- Determine roles for other stakeholders in the Scrum environment
- Explore some of the rules about Scrum

The Product Owner

The Product Owner has a very important role in Scrum. The Product Owner provides business knowledge and is responsible for the value that the team creates. The Product Owner does this through prioritizing the list of items that the team works on, called the Product Backlog. The Product Owner is also responsible for answering questions, making decisions and coordinating the requirements from multiple stakeholders (if applicable).

The key responsibilities of the Product Owner could be summarized as follows:

- Brings business knowledge and acumen

- Owns and prioritize the Product Backlog
- Gets answers for the team and makes decisions
- Ensures that the team delivers business value and provides return on investment
- Plans product strategy and releases
- Provides progress reports to leadership, where required

My favorite analogy for the Product Owner is my own son, Jack. When he was eight years old, we took him to a nice beach resort for Spring Break. One of the first days we were there, Jack wanted to have a Pina Colada by the pool. And if you are like me, you know that even a non-alcoholic version of that drink costs nearly $10 delivered poolside, before the service charge and tip. I squirmed, I resisted, and I fought back. What else could I do? We were going to go broke! "Wouldn't you rather have a souvenir", I cajoled, "something to remember the trip by?"

Fortunately, my wife often shows more wisdom than I do. She suggested that we set a spending budget for my son, that we actually give this 8 year old $10 per day to spend any way he wanted. It was pure brilliance! After we made that decision, I let go of control. I no longer had to worry about the money, there was a set amount and he was free to spend it however he wanted.

FIGURE 7.1 – MY 8-YEAR OLD PRODUCT OWNER

And so it goes with the Product Owner. The Product Owner makes the decisions on how to spend their money by prioritizing the backlog that the team will work on. The Product Owner chooses to invest in those areas that he or she thinks will return the most value. The team in turn does not worry about the priorities. The team focuses on what they do best, the work itself. You could say that the Product Owner determines the "what" and the team determines the "how". Outside of helping to prioritize for technical dependencies or risk, the team leaves the prioritization to the Product Owner.

Good Product Owners

What makes a Product Owner a good Product Owner? A good Product Owner knows the business and makes good and timely decisions on priorities to keep the team productive. They also encourage and challenge the team, creating a virtuous and self-reinforcing cycle.

How much time does it take the Product Owner to do their job? That depends on how many teams they are supporting and on the availability of subject matter experts. I've seen the Product Owner spend nearly all their time supporting a team; they attended all the

Scrum meetings and acted as part of the team. In other cases, the Product Owner attended only the Sprint Planning 1 meeting and the Sprint Review. They spent some time on Product Backlog prioritization and refinement, but they did not act as part of the team and had a full time job elsewhere. Their Scrum responsibilities took about 2-3 hours per week.

Some of the common ways that organizations flounder when selecting Product Owners are outlined in Roman Pichler's excellent book, *Agile Product Management with Scrum*.

- **Underpowered Product Owners** – Underpowered Product Owners don't have the authority to make decisions.
- **Overworked Product Owners** – Overworked Product Owners don't have the time to spend with the team. This can be due to supporting too many teams, or because the Product Owners have been given too many responsibilities.
- **Partial Product Owners** – The partial Product Owner results when the organization splits the role among multiple people.
- **Distant Product Owners** – The distant Product Owner works separately from the team, by geography and/or time zones.
- **Proxy Product Owners** – A proxy is a person acting on behalf of another. In the Product Owner role, this is most common when the Product Owner is too busy or too distant to engage with the team on a regular basis.
- **Product Owner Committees** – The Product Owner is intended to be a single person for a reason – so that there is one set of priorities for the team. When the Product Owner role is distributed among multiple people, you have a Product Owner committee. A committee is not the optimal solution, but it can be made to work if one person is the ultimate decision-maker. Generally speaking, the team cannot serve multiple masters. (Pichler, 2010)

I recently did a quick review of 20 of the Product Owners I've worked with and looked for some of these common mistakes, or anti-patterns. Though not a scientific study, it does provide some support to Pichler's findings (see * items below), as well as some additional things to watch for.

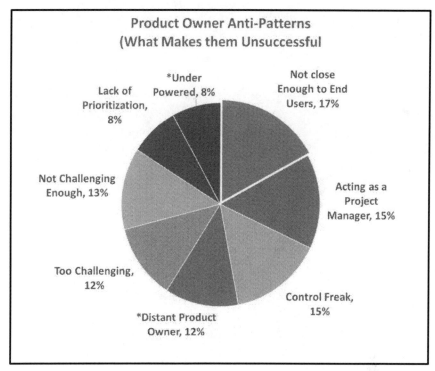

FIGURE 7.2 – PROJECT OWNER ANTI-PATTERNS

Some of the survey results reflected in the chart above are quite obvious. If the Product Owner is not close to the end users, or if they are not co-located with the team, then that will slow things down or introduce issues. Clearly it will be difficult to have Product Owners, end users, and the team all in one place. It does happen. If I had to choose between having the Product Owner close to the end users or close to the team, it is probably more important that they are close to the team, enabling face to face meetings. Product Owners that have the luxury of being co-located with the team are more likely to have a positive and reciprocal relationship with the team. On the other hand, if Product Owners don't understand the work that the end users are doing, they may not prioritize correctly resulting in a product or solution that the end users will not need.

You might find that "Acting as a project manager" and "Control Freak" are somewhat surprising anti-patterns. In practice, there are some activities that the traditional project manager would do that the Product Owner is responsible for. This includes planning releases. Beyond that, managing tasks, directing the team, or providing estimates are all activities that are not the responsibility of the Product Owner. Product Owners that try to control everything beyond the priorities and the release will often stifle creativity and foster resentment from the team.

It may surprise you to see that I have anti-patterns for both "too challenging" and "not challenging enough". There is a healthy tension for the Product Owner to be somewhat challenging and asking for more from the team. However, the Product Owner should be "asking" for more and not "demanding" it. If a Product Owner is too demanding, they send the message to the team that they are not good enough or that they are not really partnering with the team. If the Product Owner is not challenging enough, they send the message that either they don't care, or they don't believe the team is up to the challenge.

Finally, the last two anti-patterns are easy to understand. The primary job of the Product Owner is prioritization, so if they are not doing that job they are failing. As an example, I supported a Product Owner that was responsible for prioritizing items that were needed to bring the organization into compliance with federal reporting regulations. There was too much work, far more than the team could ever accomplish. The Product Owner would shrug and say, "It all needs to get done", or, "it is all top priority". This is not helpful to a team.

The Scrum Master

The key responsibilities of the Scrum Master include:

- Master Scrum, and teach it to the team and Product Owner
- Serve as a coach to help the team self-organize
- Facilitate
- Apply systems thinking to help the team improve
- Identify and remove impediments to team productivity
- Serve the team

Just as the name sounds, the Scrum Master is responsible for mastering Scrum. They are to learn Scrum, and teach it to the team, the Product Owner, and other stakeholders. The goal is skillful application of the Scrum framework so that the team is highly productive.

As a coach, the Scrum Master helps the team to self-organize. This is not as simple as telling them go get organized. Instead, the Scrum Master observes the team and offers feedback. The Scrum Master looks in from outside the team and helps them to see their strengths and weaknesses. The Scrum Master effectively holds up a mirror so that the team can accurately see themselves. Good Scrum Masters also help the team to make choices about how to improve. Good coaches help people and teams figure things out for themselves, and get better on their own. They leave the team feeling positive.

For this reason, questions are a key tool in the Scrum Master's toolkit. A question that I ask frequently when coaching is, "do you want feedback?" Another question that I like is, "what do you think you should do?"

Good questions challenge assumptions, inspire creativity and fresh ideas, and generate learning. There is an entire study around these good questions called powerful questions. (Vogt, n.d.) Some examples of powerful questions are shown below.

- If you could change anything about this [team, situation, project, etc.], what would it be?
- What holds you back from performing at your best?
- What could happen that would enable you or the team to feel fully engaged and energized about (your specific situation)?

The Scrum Master is also responsible for facilitating some of the team meetings. Initially the Scrum Master may facilitate all team meetings, though this is something that he or she should teach the team to do as quickly as possible. However, the Scrum Master should continue to facilitate the retrospective. The Scrum Master is the best facilitator for this meeting because they are not directly engaged in doing the work every day, and they can bring a more balanced view of the work. The Sprint Retrospective meeting is a critical part of inspecting and adapting and is a valuable tool for team improvement.

Another important responsibility of the Scrum Master is to remove impediments to team productivity, while teaching the team to remove impediments. An impediment is anything that impedes productivity. Most team members are good at analysis, development or testing. Few team members excel at chasing down the purchase order for new equipment, locating the right SME for a particular function, or resolving conflicts with the Product Owner. The Scrum Master asks or listens for impediments and then goes to work helping the team resolve those things that they cannot effectively solve for themselves.

The best Scrum Masters are systems thinkers, with an interest in organizational design. They see some of the underlying root causes of the impediments that occur and they work to fix the system. They are open, transparent and honest about the organizational impediments and recommendations for improvement.

The Scrum Master may do a number of other things for the team, especially with a new team. They may create and maintain a burndown chart, organize the task board, and track velocity. Over time, the team should be taught how to do these things.

Finally, the Scrum Master serves the team by doing whatever they can to help them be more productive.

Scrum Masters are Not Project Managers

As mentioned earlier, the Scrum Master job is different than the job of project manager and requires different skills to be successful. In fact, most Agilists would recommend against using project managers as Scrum Masters. But you can see from the blending of roles in job postings (i.e. Project Manager / Scrum Master) that people are not paying attention to that recommendation! The table below shows some of the key differences between the two roles:

Project Manager	Scrum Master
• Responsible for the budget, schedule and scope	• Responsible for helping the team to self-organize
• Assigns tasks, tracks them to completion	• Removes impediments
• Communicates to all stakeholders	• Stays out of the way
• Controls the project	• Teaches the team and product owner Scrum
• "Single throat to choke"	• Servant leader

FIGURE 7.3 - THE PROJECT MANAGER VS. THE SCRUM MASTER

It is unfortunate but some organizations equate the two roles and swap people between them. And in other companies, the project managers had no choice but to volunteer for the Scrum Master positions since they were told there was no role for project managers in the new Agile organization. Desperation and scarcity are not good reasons for wanting to be a Scrum Master!

I've actually seen project managers take on the Scrum Master role and then fail, as predicted. On the other hand, I have worked with other project managers who, with proper training and coaching, are able to perform well as Scrum Masters. It is very much an individual thing.

So where do Scrum Masters Come From?

The Scrum Master is one of the most important roles, and often the most difficult to fill on a team. Conventional wisdom is to leverage internal candidates for this role. The argument goes that people who are already involved are best positioned to understand how the organization works and get things done.

On the other hand, I've seen external Scrum Masters come into an organization and operate very effectively. One thing that an external candidate brings is new ideas. They also may find themselves free of limitations about what can and cannot be done, and less willing to accept "that's the way things are done around here". Moving to empowered and self-organizing teams is a big mental shift, and the Scrum Master needs to drive that. So I have found that external Scrum Masters can be effective.

So how do we go about determining who wants to be the Scrum Master? If an organization has no Scrum Masters as they begin implementing Scrum, what do they do? Do they simply hang out a "help wanted" sign?

When looking at organizations, I've found the best role to transition into the Scrum Master role is the business analyst. This may be in part because they've not been the "boss" or felt they were held accountable for projects like the project manager might feel. In fact, one of the best Scrum Masters I coached was first a business analyst, she did some test automation, and she was a CPA working in a financial services firm. She had the skills to wear many hats, and could help the team in many ways.

Developing Scrum Masters from Internal Candidates

New Scrum Masters cannot simply read a book or attend one training class and expect to be effective. What is generally effective is a combination of training and coaching. Individuals need someone they can huddle with before and after key meetings where they can plan, try some things out and then get immediate feedback.

But Scrum Masters also need to hit the books. The range of topics that Scrum Masters need to master ranges from Agile, Scrum and technical practices, to books on people and self-directed teams, and a host of other topics. One Agile trainer claimed that there were 75 books that Scrum Masters should have read! My own recommendation is something less – perhaps 15 books. See Appendix C for a recommended reading list for Scrum Masters.

Examples of Growing Scrum Masters – Large Financial Services Firm

In one organization I coached, the leadership decided that they would start with one full time Scrum Master for each of the seven teams they were forming. They asked for volunteers, and they offered information sessions about what the role entailed. The seven volunteers were from a variety of roles:

- Two were currently first line managers
- Two were project managers

- Two were in quality assurance / testing roles
- One was a developer

I worked with the seven teams and facilitated a process where they chose the Scrum Master that would support them. It was a difficult process as several teams wanted the same person to serve them. However, after teams had a Scrum Master they began working together as an Agile team, and I coached the Scrum Masters.

After six months, all but two of these new Scrum Masters moved to other roles because they didn't have the skill sets needed to effectively help the teams self-organize and deliver working software. I worked closely throughout the process with the leadership team to gather feedback about how the Scrum Masters were doing. The biggest determinate for how the Scrum Master was doing was how the team was doing.

It was one of the line managers and one of the project managers who 'made the cut' so to speak. If I had to name the characteristics that made these two successful, it would be a focus on delivering working software, courage, facilitation skills and an openness to coaching and training.

Examples of Growing Scrum Masters – Small Consulting Firm

In another small organization I supported, there were no obvious internal candidates for Scrum Master so they were looking outside. The person they found through their own contacts, was not a former Scrum Master or project manager. In fact, this individual had no software development experience at all. His background? He was trained as a pastor! And after training and coaching, he did quite well! He leveraged the leadership and facilitation skills that he had developed over the years, including servant leadership, to become an effective Scrum Master.

The Team

In Scrum, the people doing the work are called the team. They may also be called the Scrum team or the Feature team. This includes developers, analysts, testers, UI designers and anyone else needed to develop the products and solutions. They are capable of taking backlog items all the way through to complete and ready for production. And they do this without relying on people outside the team. To be effective, Scrum teams must have the following characteristics:

- Cross functional
- Correct Team Size
- Full-time Assigned to One Team
- Co-Located
- Focused
- Self-Organizing

We will look at each of these characteristics in the sections that follow.

Cross Functional

Effective Scrum teams are cross functional, that is, they have all the skills needed to complete the work in the backlog. A team consisting solely of Java developers or Web Designers would not have all the skills needed to complete the work. It is more likely for a team to have 3-4 developers, a business analyst and a testing specialist. The team needs to have all the skills necessary to complete the backlog items.

In the previous example, it might be more appropriate to say that you have 3-4 people with development as their "primary skillset". These developers would be deep in a development tool such as Java or Python, but would also be growing other secondary skillsets needed for their work, including testing, business analysis and understanding the business domain. In practice, team members have what is referred to as "T-Shaped" skill sets. They are deep in one particular area, but they are broad in many other areas. Team members teach their primary skillset to other team members, and they learn new secondary skills from others. This concept of learning across functions and broadening is what Takeuchi and Nonaka called multi-learning. (Takeuchi, 1986)

The cross training and multi-learning results in the elimination of specialists. Specialists are a problem on Scrum teams because they create bottlenecks. When we have only one person who understands the automated test scripts, or is the fastest at Java development, we inadvertently create a constraint within the team. As Craig Larman said in his Scrum Master Certification Course:

> *"If your first name is fast, your middle name is bottleneck"*
>
> *--Craig Larman*

The idea of avoiding specialists on Scrum teams may be particularly troublesome to some individuals. Some individuals have spent their career striving to be the one with the best understanding of Ruby, or the only who gets the SQL queries. They have tried to build a sense of job security by being the go to guy or girl. They have created what leadership would call a key man risk. With Scrum, we strive to reduce or eliminate the key risk by cross training and encouraging cross-functional teams.

Correct Team Size

We have talked about composition of the team. Now let's talk about the team size. The Scrum Guide lists the optimal Scrum team to be between 3-9 people. When teams have less than 3 people, there is insufficient critical mass to complete the work. More than 9, and the organization and coordination become burdensome and inefficient.

Others use the rule of 7 +/- 2 as an optimal team size. Mike Cohn recommends the rule used at Amazon that the team should be sized so that two pizzas will feed them. (Cohn, 2009)

Full-Time Assigned to One Team

Another critical aspect of the Scrum team is that they are full-time assigned to one team. This concept may be difficult for most project managers and organizations to swallow. Most organizations have grown accustomed to over allocating people to projects and starting way too many projects at once. This comes at the cost of significant overhead in terms of project managers and PMO staff who run around and track what people are working on to make sure everyone is fully utilized. With Scrum teams, people are assigned to just one team and the organization strives to keep that team intact for the long term.

Co-Located

Another aspect to Scrum teams is that they work together, ideally in one room and sitting at one table. They are co-located. Scrum teams work together as a unit. Everyone is pretty much aware of the status of all the items because they are all together.

When you have people working together in one room, you get what Alistair Cockburn calls osmotic communications. Everyone can pretty much hear every conversation. As listeners we can selectively tune in or out of conversations, depending on our level of interest or the importance of the topic. Teams that work together in one room get the benefit of everyone knowing what is going on. Distributed teams cannot come anywhere close to this level of communication and collaboration.

Teams that are co-located need to provide space and facilities for individual work as well. This could be for making a private phone call, or it could be for thinking. Most organizations that make use of team rooms also provide small cubicles, private offices, or even phone booths for individual work.

Many organizations today make use of distributed teams to lower costs, get access to additional skills not available locally, or to provide additional team capacity. When they move to Scrum, these organizations are encouraged to review their distributed teams, and try to re-organize to create co-located teams. Rather than have several teams distributed across multiple locations, they create co-located teams in each location. This may be disruptive and costly in the short run, but it is better than maintaining distributed teams over the long haul.

In a study of distributed team productivity, Jeff Sutherland concluded that it is possible to create a distributed team that was just as productive as a co-located team but only if conscious and adequate compensation is made for the loss of face-to-face communications. (Sutherland, et al., 2009)

Distributed teams will not be as productive as co-located teams unless communications are made a top priority. Instant messaging tools and webcams can help and should be leveraged to their greatest extent.

Focused

Focus is closely related to the two previous items, full time assigned and co-located. Scrum teams are in an environment where team members are focused on the work of the team. They are not working on other projects, or on their own personal business. Nor are they doing a lot of social loafing or goldbricking.

The idea of having team members focused may seem obvious, but unfortunately it is not always common practice. Many organizations today foster practices that prevent or reduce ability to focus. We overschedule people or have meetings that lack purpose, agendas, or are not timeboxed. We assign people to multiple projects or give them conflicting goals or unachievable deadlines. Scrum can help protect against this, as we will see when we talk about the rules of Scrum in the next section.

Even Scrum teams can suffer from lack of focus. I was once the temporary Scrum Master for a Scrum team that was struggling to deliver on a troubled project that was being transitioned from traditional development to Scrum. When I recommended that we all move into an available work room and sit together, some team members were enthusiastic while others were resistant. However, once the enthusiastic ones made the move, everyone moved in. Within the first day, I discovered that one of the contractors on the team was spending an hour each day on a conference call for a project for another client company! This is just one minor example of how working together in one room brings focus.

One thing that helps with focus is having large and visible displays of the team's work and progress. The most important of these is the task board. The task board is hard to ignore, and will easily show whether or not the team is focused. The Scrum Master is responsible for helping the team to create and maintain these tools.

Self-Organizing

Agile teams are self-organizing. This is one of the 12 Agile principles that we covered in Chapter 1.

> *"The best architectures, requirements, and designs*
> *emerge from self-organizing teams." (Cunningham, 2001)*

What exactly does self-organizing mean? Self-organizing means that they don't have someone outside the team – a functional manager or project manager – to tell them what to do. The team collectively plans their work and organizes themselves. Operating within the constraints of the Scrum framework, they have control over their work and how it gets done. This is the ideal view of Scrum, though most organizations fall short of allowing full self-organization.

I've personally seen ranges of self-organization, even within the same organization. Some teams that I coached at a large financial services organization had nearly complete autonomy and say over their work. They even got to choose which team they worked on and by implication, which product they would support and development technology they would employ. These teams had no line managers directing them, and were left to organize themselves however they thought best. The individual people on the team got to choose a line "coach" who would support them in their career, but they did not have anyone who was a boss. At the end of the year, these teams provided each other 360 degree feedback, rather than having a supervisor review them.

Other teams within that same organization had very little autonomy and ability to self-organize. Their line manager chose to participate in every Scrum meeting, asking questions and directing the team on what to do. The line manager would also have frequent one-on-one meetings with each team member. These team members had no doubt who was in control of the team.

I found most teams fall somewhere in between these two extremes. Frequently there is some form of line management who is charged with overseeing the team. Whatever that level of oversight, teams are able to exercise more control over their ability to self-organize and self-manage.

What I've described in the sections above are the ideal characteristics of a Scrum team. If you don't have co-located teams, you can still do Scrum. If your team members are not 100% dedicated, you can still do Scrum. You can do Scrum in any situation; you just have to recognize that your team is not going to be as productive as it would be with the ideal characteristics.

Other Stakeholders

Now that we have discussed the 3 primary roles in Scrum, what about any other people who are involved with the Scrum team? Do they have a role in Scrum?

Anyone that is outside of the three Scrum roles is considered either a subject matter expert or a stakeholder to the process and not directly involved with Scrum. In fact, the Scrum framework makes a clear distinction between those who are committed to the completion of work, and those that are just interested or involved. This is commonly conveyed by the story of the pig and chicken.

As the story goes, the pig and chicken have agreed to start a breakfast restaurant together. The chicken agrees to provide the eggs, and the pig agrees to provide the bacon. The pig is **committed** to the restaurant, while the chicken is only **involved.**

As it relates to Scrum, the Product Owner, the Scrum Master and the team are like the pigs; they are committed. Everyone else is just involved, like the chicken. For example, line managers and other leaders are described as chickens. This means that they are not on the line for the results. I've heard variations of this story to include roosters – executive management.

This is a really important concept. In one organization I worked in, there were significant financial bonuses provided for important projects that were completed, and often negative attention to participants of projects that failed in some way. As one could imagine, this led to a number of suboptimal team behaviors. First, there were a surprising number of people jockeying to be "involved" in every project, on the off-chance that the project might succeed. At the same time these involved parties kept a safe distance from all projects in case they failed. The cost of carrying all that extra dead weight probably didn't help any of the projects.

When I arrived to coach the very first team on the use of Agile, I was surprised to find nearly a dozen people in the room. Could these all be part of the same team I wondered? As it turned out, there were some managers and other chickens in the room. They expected to be included in the Scrum team, even though they didn't really plan on doing any work. I had several heart to heart discussions with a number of them before we could winnow the team down to 8 working members.

Scrum is not for Everyone

In the work that I have done helping organizations adopt Scrum, I have found that it isn't for everyone. Some people don't have skillsets that the teams need, and are unwilling to cross train. Others, seem to fall into two categories: they are uncomfortable working closely with others, or, they thrive on individual heroics.

In a Scrum team, there is absolutely no hiding out – everyone can pretty much see all the work done by others. If you are not productive, or if you are hiding out, Scrum will make that visible.

For those that thrive on individual heroics, Scrum will be an unwelcome change. With the constant pace and regular cadence of delivery, there is no incentive to take risks or encourage heroics. Additionally, it is the team that gets credit for work that is well done, and not an individual.

It has been my experience that while 9 in 10 individuals thrive in the transition to Scrum, 1 in 10 do not do so well for the two main reasons above. This has been a consistent finding for me over the years.

Where Did the Project Manager Responsibilities Go?

The responsibilities that would normally be handled by a project manager are generally still done by Scrum teams. So who does them? The chart below is a high-level breakout of the traditional roles that a PM would do.

Project Manager	Product Owner	Scrum Master	Team
Planning Product Strategy and Releases	✓		
Planning Iterations			✓
Planning Tasks			✓
Progress/Status Reporting to Leadership	✓		
Clearing Roadblocks	✓	✓	✓
Task Planning & Tracking			✓
Managing Risks	✓		✓
Prioritizing Work	✓		
Select Resources for the Team			✓

FIGURE 7.4 - THE PROJECT MANAGEMENT RESPONSIBILITIES AND THE SCRUM TEAM

The Rules of Scrum

As we have mentioned several times, Scrum is a simple framework with very few rules. I will share with you some of the written rules as well as some that are practiced but not necessarily written everywhere.

There are actually very few written rules for Scrum. The Scrum Guide lists a couple of them explicitly, though many more are baked into the process and not written out. The rules primarily serve to protect the team from unnecessary interruption, and to foster self-organization of the team. Here are some of the rules I have worked with, read, or been taught over the years:

- The Scrum team is self-organizing; no one outside the team tells them what to do.
- Developer teams are cross-functional. They have all the skills needed to create a potentially shippable product increment.
- There are no sub teams within the team; all tasks are owned by everyone and there are no handoffs.
- Only team members participate in the daily Scrum. I have also seen this rule stated as only those who have tasks may speak at the daily Scrum. This would include Product Owner and Scrum Master updates.
- There are no titles for team members, other than developer, regardless of the work they perform.
- The Product Owner prioritizes the backlog.
- The team alone decides how much work they will take on in any given iteration, based on their capacity.
- The team is responsible for estimation.
- Everyone needs to honor the iteration timeframe. No one is allowed to change the timeframe for the iteration.
- The sprint should not be interrupted, nor should the team be interrupted and asked to work on other things.
- The scope of the iteration may not be changed by anyone; the only exception is the team who may decide to pull in backlog items if they find they have excess capacity, or they may choose to stop work on an item if the Product Owner decides it is no longer needed.
- The team accepts work; the Product Owner doesn't and cannot force it on the team.

- The team agrees to getting stories all the way to "done" (i.e. potentially shippable or ready for release to customer) at the end of the iteration.
- The team works with the Product Owner to maintain a release plan that reflects likely delivery of the release, based on the team's velocity.

Chapter 7 Summary

- Scrum has three roles for participants, the Scrum Master, the Product Owner and the team. Everyone else is considered a stakeholder.
- For a Scrum team to be productive, each of the three roles must be properly staffed.
- Scrum has very few rules. These rules protect the team and encourage self-organization.

Chapter 8: Scrum Meetings

Key Takeaways for Chapter 8

By the end of Chapter 8, you will be able to:

- Discuss the four meetings used as part of the Scrum Framework
- Provide tips for success on each meeting
- Provide an example calendar for a 2-week iteration length

Overview

The Scrum framework includes a set of four distinct meetings as highlighted in the diagram below. These are sometimes called events, ceremonies or rituals, depending on the organization or trainer. They are the Sprint Planning meetings part 1 and 2, the daily Scrum or standup, the Sprint Review and the Sprint Retrospective. There are a couple of other unofficial meetings that we will cover in this Chapter as well.

FIGURE 8. 1 - THE MEETINGS OF SCRUM

The purpose of having a standard set of meetings is to reduce waste and increase productivity by giving the team a uniform and predictable process. All of the Scrum meetings are timeboxed with the meeting length proportional to the length of the sprint. The exception to this is the daily Scrum meeting which is always 15 minutes or less. These meetings form a cadence for communication and completion and help to keep the team on track. Each of these meetings is described in detail in the sections that follow.

Sprint Planning Meetings

Project managers will feel right at home in the Sprint Planning meeting. The purpose of the meeting is to plan in detail the work to be completed in the next sprint. The meeting is generally split into two parts, each with a different focus. The total timebox for Sprint Planning is 2 hours per week of sprint.

Sprint Planning 1

In Sprint Planning 1, the Scrum team and the Product Owner work together to determine the list of backlog items or user stories that will be taken on by the team in the sprint. The focus in sprint planning is getting agreement with the Product Owner on the stories, or "what" is to be developed. This meeting is the first meeting in the new sprint, and is usually close to the end of the previous sprint, so the Product

Owner and team are usually familiar with the backlog items that were completed in the last iteration. The Product Owner will typically have a good idea of what they want, based on their prioritized backlog. He or she works with the team to select the top priority items from the Product Backlog that roughly matches the sprint velocity or capacity of the team. Note that new teams will have to guess their capacity for the first sprint, as discussed in Chapter 5. The Product Owner makes an offer of those backlog items to the team.

Though it is not required, it is recommended that the team and Product Owner discuss the high priority items at this time. The team will often ask questions to confirm their understanding of each item. The team may even suggest an item to be included in the sprint due to technical dependencies, risk, or because it is an engineering or maintenance activity that the Product Owner may not be aware of. The backlog items are rarely ever new or unknown; teams should be working with the Product Owner on refining or grooming backlog items on a regular basis. However, it is possible that the Product Owner brings a new, top priority item to the Sprint Planning 1 meeting, and the team will discuss whether or not they have sufficient information to take it on within the sprint.

While the Product Owner will want the team to take on as much as possible, the Product Owner and team will quickly realize that there is no point in offering more to the team than the team has the capacity to take on. Team capacity is not based on hope or wishful thinking; it is based on historical velocity and the total time the team will have to work on items. If there are known company holidays, extraordinary product support requirements, or any other event likely to reduce team capacity, this may also be discussed at this time.

The Product Owner and team will generally discuss and agree on a sprint goal, which is a short statement of achievement for the team for the coming sprint. An example might be to prove out a certain search technology, or to complete all the stories needed to comply with the trade reporting requirements in Dodd-Frank legislation. Not all teams leverage the concept of the sprint goal, but those that do tend to have more focus.

Once the Product Owner offers the backlog items, and the team has had their questions answered, Sprint Planning 1 is ended and the team focuses on Sprint Planning 2.

It is common for multiple teams to work with the same Product Owner and pull stories from the same backlog. In this case, Sprint Planning 1 is conducted as a joint meeting, with the teams working together with the Product Owner to earmark the backlog items they are likely to take on in Sprint Planning 2.

Sprint Planning 2

In Sprint Planning 2, the team works together to plan in detail the work required to bring all the items that were offered by the Product Owner to "done". The Product Owner is not required to attend Sprint Planning 2, though it is highly recommended so that the team doesn't get delayed waiting for an answer to a question. If the Product Owner is not physically present, they should make themselves available via phone or instant messaging.

The concept of getting items all the way to "done" in a sprint is a critical part of planning. Teams need to know everything that must be done to complete the items and plan all that work within the sprint. As mentioned in Chapter 7, most teams will create a definition of done list and hang it in their team area or team room. It is a handy reference for sprint planning. Teams can confirm that they have all the work addressed, and nothing was left out. An example is shown below.

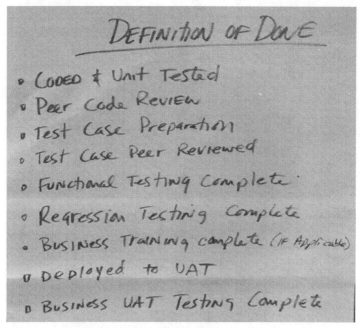

FIGURE 8. 2 - DEFINITION OF DONE EXAMPLE

The flow of Sprint Planning 2 is that the team first determines their collective capacity, then they work together to plan the items in detail, starting with the first item. They plan out the development, testing, analysis, user testing (if needed) and anything else needed to complete the item. Rather than using a divide and conquer approach, everyone participates in the planning process so that everyone on the team understands each item. This approach can seem slow or wasteful since it can take up to 3-4 hours to plan out the work for a 2-week sprint. However, this investment up front pays off later in the sprint when the team is striving to complete the items using their available resources.

The process for determining capacity can be very simple. The team starts by determining the hours that they will be able to dedicate to the work of the sprint. Some teams use a simple formula like 6 hours per day of the sprint per person, subtracting any holidays or vacation days. Others use a more elaborate, person by person approach for each day (see diagram below). Other teams take it a step further and estimate refinement time, time spent on production support and time spent on technical or engineering backlog items. It is up to each team to determine the approach that they want to use to plan their capacity, so that they take on the appropriate amount of work.

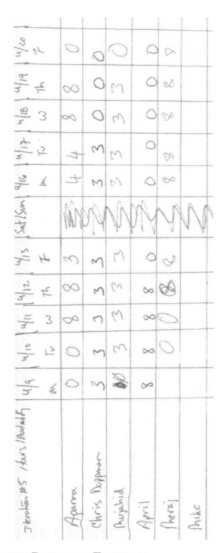

FIGURE 8. 3 - CAPACITY PLANNING EXAMPLE

I like to take a relatively simple approach to capacity planning as shown in the diagram above. I pass around a piece of paper with a matrix on it. The days of the 2-week sprint form the columns, and the team members' names form the rows. I let each person write in the hours per day that they can contribute to the sprint. In an ideal world everyone is available full time, however, there are frequently reasons that they cannot be. Team members may be out of the office, have non-team meetings to attend, production support responsibilities, communities of practice meetings to lead, or other time that cannot be spent on the sprint.

Once everyone completes their work, I attach this piece of paper to the sprint burndown. Could this chart be in Excel? Sure! But then we need to work out how people will update it and that usually would mean that one person is using a laptop and projector and they interrogate each person and the whole process takes 15 minutes. I find that passing the sheet of paper in the meeting takes very little time and people can fill it out as we go.

Once teams have a total capacity in hours for the sprint, they begin planning out the tasks for each of the backlog items, one item at a time. They talk through the item, and then work together to determine what tasks are required to complete the item to done. A handy reference is the team's definition of done, which is used as a checklist for the required tasks. The team lists out all the tasks for each item, and then works together to estimate the hours that it will take to complete each task.

Generally, tasks should be small – less than a day – in order to provide a granular enough tracking of the work. Tasks that are big tend to get started and not finished and become unpredictable. Teams should break big tasks down into 2 or 4 hours. This also makes it easier to monitor progress because tasks that are less than a day should move from in progress to done from one daily Scrum meeting to another. The task hours are generally based on how long on average any member of the team will take to complete the items. Teams frequently pair up on tasks, and that is sometimes marked on the task.

It is important to note that it is the team, and only the team that estimates the size of the tasks for a sprint. Approaches for task estimates vary. Some teams plan the tasks together and others divide and conquer, letting individuals plan the tasks. Some teams even use "planning poker" to get agreement on the estimated hours to complete a particular task. The downside of having an individual do the estimates is that they may not reflect the time that it would take the average team member to do the work. And I discourage teams from assigning work to one individual during sprint planning. By pre-assigning work, we create sub-optimization and bottlenecks. Rather, teams are encouraged to leave work unassigned, and for team members to pick up the next most important task when they have availability.

I have seen teams use a divide and conquer approach during sprint planning where each person, or sometimes a pair, take on a story or two and then plan it out. They share the results with the team at the end of the meeting. While this may be faster overall, I don't recommend this approach as it tends to create silos and specialization. Teams that have these silos are less likely to achieve their goals because they are not "swarming", the process where everyone works together to accomplish items as quickly as possible.

Sprint Planning as a Cross-Training Exercise

The collaborative nature of group planning is helpful as a training exercise. A couple of teams that I coached recently used this approach. One team had experience on a particular backlog while the other did not. The two teams sat together in a conference room for Sprint Planning 2, and planned out the tasks for each backlog item, one item at a time, with both teams working together. It felt painfully slow – the first item took 45 minutes! However, subsequent items went more quickly and the cross training was powerful. Even with 12 people in the room, the conversations were effective in getting the second team up to speed.

Sprint Planning Anti-Patterns

One behavior that I have often noted with new teams is a reluctance to engage in Sprint Planning 2. They will often want to leave the team or meeting room and work alone. I've seen this enough times to anticipate it and help teams work through it. I believe it is a lack of familiarity with team planning, and a fear of looking dumb that leads to this. Let's face it, planning can be hard work. Individuals don't want to be put on the spot or look ignorant about an item, or about how the existing system works. So I often see this desire to leave the meeting, and go do planning alone. Don't do it! Planning together is a way to share knowledge and keep everyone on the same page. Acknowledge what is actually happening in the room, how different and awkward it feels. And then push on.

I've come to expect this new-team-joint-planning behavior now that I have observed it enough times. But early in my tenure as an Agile coach I witnessed (and didn't stop) planning meetings that dragged on for hours and hours longer than necessary. I witnessed teams who would spend a full 8-hour day on the planning. They were working separately, on stories that were not refined for the sprint. Fortunately Scrum sets a timebox of 4 hours for sprint planning. As one of my favorite Agile trainers would say, it is illegal to violate the timebox. Now, I anticipate the resistance to team planning, and I help teams work through it. I help them to work with the Product Owner to prepare stories in advance so that they have the information they need to plan the items. And I enforce the timebox – when the time is up, that is all the planning that can be done.

As they plan stories, the team checks back against their team capacity in hours – they stop planning if they have no more capacity to take on stories. The outputs of the sprint planning process include the team's commitment of backlog items, the sprint goal, the team capacity in hours and the detailed tasks needed to complete the items in the sprint. Some teams send an email to the Product Owner that includes their forecast of items to be completed in the sprint. If the Product Owner participates in Sprint Planning 2, this is unnecessary.

The backlog items and the detailed tasks are typically placed on a whiteboard or wall to create a physical task board. This is a form of visual management that is simple, easy to maintain and provides a clear indication of team status. The task board typically contains three columns- "not started", in progress and done. The detailed tasks that the team creates are placed in the "not started" column, and then team members will move them to in progress when they are ready to work on them.

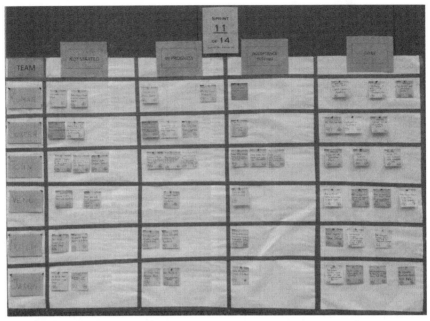

FIGURE 8. 4 - A TASKBOARD

Teams will usually draft a burndown chart at the end of sprint planning. A burndown chart is a very simple chart showing a comparison of the team's capacity over the course of the sprint, as well as the work remaining in front of the team. The purpose is to provide a reliable indicator to the team if they are on track to meet their goals for the sprint. Unlike traditional status reports, where the items are often considered green right up until they are late and turn red, the consistent use of the burndown chart can provide a reliable view of the team's progress vs. their goals for the sprint.

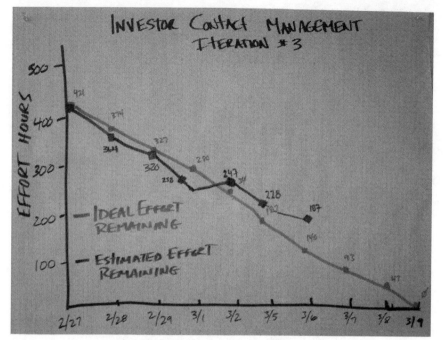

FIGURE 8. 5 - A SAMPLE BURNDOWN CHART

An example of a burndown chart is shown above. The red line represents an ideal line of the team's completion of work, while the blue line represents the actual work remaining. This work remaining is estimated at the end of sprint planning, and then updated every work day of the sprint.

5 Tips for Effective Sprint Planning Meetings

1. **Be Realistic** - The Product Owner should offer items to the team that are roughly equivalent to the team's capacity.
2. **Small and Evenly-Sized Work** - Teams should work with the Product Owner to break down Product Backlog items to be 1/3 of a sprint or less. Smaller, more consistently sized backlog items will be easier to plan and complete, reduce variability and increase team productivity and predictability.
3. **Teams Estimate** - Team members are responsible for estimating the tasks required to complete each backlog item. Teams should also break down tasks to be two to eight hours. Like small backlog items, small tasks are easier to estimate,

track and complete. Teams will have a better sense of progress and accomplishment if they see that they are completing tasks.

4. **Whole Team** - Teams should work together to plan as a team, rather than taking a divide and conquer approach.

5. **Burn Down** – Use the burndown chart to show the work remaining for the sprint. It will allow the team to track whether they are on course, and provide an early indication to the Product Owner if an item is not going to be completed.

The Daily Scrum

The daily Scrum or daily standup meeting is a short daily meeting used by the team to plan and coordinate their efforts. It is timeboxed to last 15 minutes and is not intended for detailed discussions. The general format is that each team member checks in by answering the following three questions:

1. What did I work on yesterday?
2. What am I going to work on today?
3. What impediments are in my way?

Note that the format of the questions above implies that the meeting is in the morning, before work has started. In practice, the daily meeting may be held at any time during the day that is convenient to the team. In particular when multiple time zones are involved, it may be at the beginning or end of the day. In that case, the questions are treated as "what have I done since we last met" and, "what will I do before we meet again".

This meeting is not a design session or detailed status meeting. If a detailed conversation is needed, it is common practice for the team or a subset of members to stay after the daily Scrum is over.

The meeting is also not an interview or interrogation. As a former project manager, I sometimes find it difficult NOT to ask questions during the standup. Some Scrum Masters may feel it is there job to interview or direct traffic in the standup- it is definitely not. It is the Scrum Masters job to make sure that the meeting happens and that it is effective. Sometimes the Scrum Master can best accomplish this by gently asking, "Who is going to kick us off?" Otherwise, the Scrum Master is best as a quiet participant, off to the side of the meeting.

The rule of thumb for the daily Scrum meeting is that while others may observe the meeting, only the pigs may speak, that is, only those team members who are committed to the project. I've also heard variations like only people who have tasks can speak – this could include the Product Owner or Scrum Master. The point is, it is not a place for a line manager or Product Owner to show up and ask questions. The intent is for the team to manage themselves.

These meetings are generally held as a standup meeting in front of the physical task board. As each person checks in, they will move their tasks from "not started" to "in progress", or from "in progress" to "done". Most teams also find it helpful to update the hours remaining for each task. At the end of the meeting, the Scrum Master or a team member will update the burndown chart with this information.

Teams that are not co-located will usually take a different approach. Most teams will adopt an online tool to support Scrum, such as VersionOne, Rally, Jira, or Trello. These tools strive to emulate the experience of having a physical task board. The tools do an OK job of showing the work. In the picture below, you can see a screenshot of a VersionOne task board. The backlog items are shown on the far left, in gray. The tasks to complete that backlog item are shown in the same row, and in either the "(none)" or "not started" column, the "In Progress", or the "Completed" column.

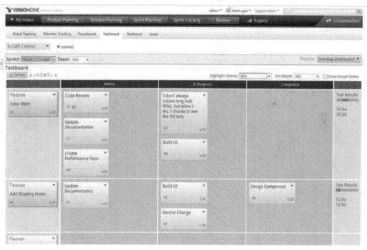

FIGURE 8. 6 - AN ONLINE TOOL TO SUPPORT SCRUM

Did I mention that I have a strong preference for a physical task board? Agile tools are one of the first things that many people new to

Agile want to focus on and it should be one of the last things they worry about. Tools can be a big distraction from being Agile. I've been through this many times with new teams. The team believes that there is some magic in using a tool to keep everyone up to date. The reality is, there is no substitute for the team to be able to walk up to the task board and see everything going on for the current sprint. You can take in the big picture, or drill in on the specifics of any one item. When teams are co-located, there is no substitute for the task board as a team communication tool and information radiator. Where possible, I strongly urge teams to use a physical task board.

When using an online tool, the format of the daily meeting may need to be altered slightly. Given the visibility of the board and the stories on it, it may be easier to go item-by-item, rather than person by person. This can be challenging for a number of reasons, not the least of which is that it becomes really difficult to have each person speak when one person is "driving" the tool on the screen. It's also much harder to keep track of what each person is working on when you go story by story. I recommend that teams that must use the virtual boards on a tool experiment with different approaches for the daily meeting.

One other caveat about the use of an online tool during daily Scrum meetings – they almost always take longer when everyone is at their desk looking at their screen. It may be that people are multi-tasking during the daily meeting. So if it has not been clear so far, let me spell it out now – I discourage the use of a tool unless it is absolutely necessary.

One more point about distributed teams – some teams find it helpful to use web cameras and lightweight video conferencing tools during the daily standup. This is particularly helpful when teams have never had the opportunity to meet face to face. Below is an example of a distributed team meeting using webcams.

FIGURE 8. 7 - A DISTRIBUTED SCRUM MEETING (PHOTO COURTESY OF THE AWESOME HONEYBADGER TEAM AT HIGHLAND SOLUTIONS)

During the Sprint, team members volunteer for work, ideally working on just one task at a time. The task should be marked to show which team member is working on it. Some teams use a sticky "South Park" character on the task to indicate that they own it, others use a colored paperclip stuck to the task while others put their initials on it. The exact form is not important; what is important is to be able to see what everyone is working on. It also helps to minimize work in progress as it will show who is working on more than one item at a time.

For example, in the chart below, the colored stickers show who is assigned to each task. They are a little hard to see, but for the work in progress, the "green" person has four tasks, the "orange" person has five tasks and the "orange X" person has five tasks. This particular team did not work together on their tasks, and had too many tasks going at the same time.

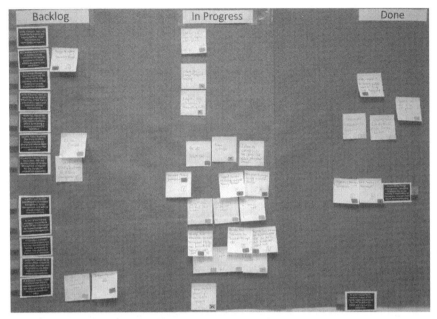

FIGURE 8. 8 - TASK ASSIGNMENTS

Though there is a daily standup to allow coordination and planning, there is no rule that team members can only take on tasks at the daily standup. In fact, it would be very ineffective to do that. Rather, the team members go back to the board and get the next task on the highest priority story. Teams aspire to a high level of cross training so that there are no specialized tasks on the board that an individual cannot take up. In practice, there are frequently tasks that either require a developer (refactor sort module) or a testing resource (run regression suite).

Team members frequently pair up to maximize learning and quality. Pair programming is an XP practice that many if not most Scrum teams have adopted. Teams represent pairing by putting multiple characters or paper clips on one tasks. They take pairing into account when estimating the work remaining.

At least once a day, usually at the daily standup, tasks are updated with a new estimate of the work remaining. The purpose of this is to track whether they can accomplish the sprint goals, and to provide early warning to the Product Owner if they cannot. The burndown is not used outside the team and teams should be under no obligation to report this to anyone outside the team.

One might assume that the burndown charts and task boards are the responsibility of the Scrum Master – this is not the case! It is the Scrum Master's responsibility to make sure that the team is organized and plans out their work. That will normally take the form of a task board and a burndown chart; however, teams may decide to experiment with other ways of accomplishing this goal. As long as the team is productive, the Scrum Master is doing their job. In any case, it is the Scrum Master's job to make sure it happens, not to do this for the team.

As a Scrum Master working with a team new to Scrum, I would usually create the visual management tools for the team for the first sprint or two, but I would quickly train the team to do this work and transition the work to the team.

This is probably a good place to talk about a role on the team that is not in the Scrum books but usually is necessary. Teams generally have one point person who is the team representative for a Sprint. The terms used include the "face" of the team, "information officer", and "information tracker". This person is responsible for making sure that the burndown charts and "tasks boards" are up to date, and they serve as a single point of contact for the Product Owner and other stakeholders. They help to avoid the situation where an email goes to the entire team and everyone ignores it or thinks someone else will address it.

Even with face of the team, teams should avoid having that face or a Scrum Master being the only person to update the task board or burndown chart. The entire team should make sure that these tools are up to date. Likewise, no one person should assign work to the team. That said, teams tend to have emergent leaders who step forward to help direct traffic for the team. They are not a boss or a manager, but their technical expertise or personality will often make them a leader on the team and someone who is respected and listed to.

Thinly Disguised Status Meetings

Several times I have coached teams where the department manager sits in on the daily meeting. It is usually a red flag that there is a lack of trust, or that the team is not really practicing self-organizing and empowered teams. In one particular case, I tried to encourage the department manager to not attend. Under the guise of "supporting the team", he would attend. Worse, when the Scrum Master left the company, this department manager sort of stepped in to take over the role. He was a Scrum Master in name only; he was first and foremost an old fashioned command and control department manager.

As a coach, I frequently find myself torn in this situation. On the one hand, his participation doesn't support the self-organizing team approach. On the other, I am trying to meet him and the team where they are. If they start there, they might eventually get to a point where the team is more effective at self-organizing and they can move the manager to a coaching or leadership role.

6 Tips for Effective Daily Scrum / Standup Meetings

Here are some tips for running an effective daily Scrum meeting.

1. **Stick to the Script** – To avoid waste, each person should answer the 3 questions listed above in the daily standup. No 'Solutioning' or 'Design Drilldowns' during the standup; any detailed discussions should follow after the meeting or have a meeting designated to discuss.

2. **One Question Rule** – Though it runs counter to my previous point, I sometimes allow for one question. What this means is, let's say Bob answers the 3 questions above, and says that yesterday he completed the GooglePlus Interface button. It may not be clear to Jay that he can start his testing so he asks a question. I have found it to be faster to allow the one question than to have Jay wait until after the standup to ask. However, I do limit it to just one question. Frequently, the first question can open a floodgate and the daily Scrum quickly turns into a longer discussion.

3. **Take Turns** – During the daily Scrum, just one person should talk at a time. Side conversations should be curtailed. Some teams use a talking token as an aid to have just one person talk.

4. **Stay Focused** – The standup is really for the team that is delivering the work. It helps to limit discussion to team

members who have tasks. Also, if you have a task, you must attend the daily Scrum or standup.

5. **Not a Status Report** – the team uses the daily meeting to inform each other and coordinate their efforts, not to provide a status report to the Scrum Master. Scrum Masters, coaches, line managers and any other observers should stand outside the circle and away from the board.

6. **Get In and Get Out** – The standup should last for no more than 15 minutes. It helps to show up on time, say what you need to say and then end the meeting.

Sprint Review

The Sprint Review is the place where the team engages with the Product Owner and business stakeholders to show them what has been built in the current sprint, and get feedback. This is a chance for the team and Product Owner to inspect and adapt the product. It is also an opportunity for the team and Product Owners to celebrate success.

If the Product Owner and stakeholders are engaged throughout the sprint (and they should be), there should be no surprises at the time of the Sprint Review.

The format of the meeting is for the team to review the list of stories to be reviewed and the team's definition of done. Then the team walks through the new functionality. Teams may ask the Product Owner if they accept the item or not – this practice is not consistently followed in my experience. There are no PowerPoint presentations, the intent is to show the new parts of the solution and how they work.

There are purists that say that this should never be called a demo though in practice I often find this to be the case. Why not a demo? The argument is that the review is when the Product Owner and stakeholders test drive the new functionality. It is not supposed to be the team showing the function; it is literally a test drive where the users provide feedback.

I understand the arguments against the demo but I am also pragmatic about it. I consider the event a showcase of the team and what it has produced. If the Product Owner understands the functions and can test drive it, terrific. If not, let the team do it.

It is important that the preparation for the Sprint Review be minimal. This is not the time to prepare PowerPoint presentations. The point is to demonstrate working solutions. So the team shows what has been built. It may require some test cases or data in order to exercise the solution, but even this should be something that was already done in the sprint, as part of the definition of done.

I've supported teams responsible for back office systems that had no way for the Product Owner or other user to test drive the system. They were tracking trades, and reporting them to regulatory agencies. The team would have to show a trade being entered, and then pull up XML files to show that the trade was correctly reported. It would have taken a pretty sophisticated Product Owner or user to be able to test drive this functionality.

On the other hand, I had a terrific Product Owner on a project that tracked client investor information in Salesforce.com. He represented a wide stakeholder base who all needed functionality from the system. He facilitated the Sprint Reviews himself, walking through the new functionality and putting the system through its paces. At the end, he would ask the stakeholders for feedback, and discuss ideas for new functions so that he could prioritize the backlog according to greatest need.

Ideas for new functionality should be translated into new stories in the backlog. I advise Product Owners to add all ideas that come out of the review. Just because they got added does not mean they will be prioritized near the top or worked on any time soon.

Like the other meetings, the Sprint Review is timeboxed at 1 hour for every week of the sprint. In my experience with teams using 2 week sprints, 2 hours is more than enough.

When you have multiple teams working together on the same project or program, it is usually preferable to have a common Sprint Review. This implies that all the teams are on the same sprint cadence. I've facilitated reviews for programs of 3, 4, 5 and 11 teams. In these cases, it is important that the review be well organized with an agenda. Each team needs to stay within a strict timebox to allow for people to join for parts of the meeting when appropriate. And of course, it is not possible to give each team 2 hours so teams work within a timebox of 20-45 minutes. These joint reviews can make for a long meeting; however, the time investment is offset by the greater sense of working together toward a common goal. It is especially important with programs that require teams to be aligned on release dates and testing.

A key question that a team should discuss with the Product Owner during the Sprint Review is 'whether or not they have developed enough functionality and should stop in a particular area. Remember that the backlog should not consist of every possible task that anyone ever thought of. The backlog represents small investments that should yield some type of business value. If we maxed out the business value in a particular area, there is no need to continue to develop more. The Product Owner should redirect the team to work on more important or valuable stories in the backlog, or potentially another backlog entirely.

7 Tips for an Effective Sprint Review

Here are some things that I have found helpful to teams in preparing for an effective Sprint Review.

1. **Get Organized in Advance** – Though it would be wasteful to spend a lot of time polishing presentations for the review, I have found that teams that invest a little time at the end of the current sprint to prepare for the Sprint Review tend to put their best foot forward. At a minimum, teams should have an agenda and a designated person to discuss the completed items. Some teams have a single person lead the entire review which provides continuity and minimizes time spent switching the project cord or asking, "Can you all see my screen now?"

2. **Take the User Perspective** – Teams should show the results from a user's point of view. Don't show code, or PowerPoint.

3. **Show the Backlog Items / User Stories first** – I have found it helpful to show the backlog item or user story first, to orient participants to the business need, before showing how the team met the need. The review is about solving that business problem and not all the technical details.

4. **Be Interesting and Relevant** – It's a show, not a code review.

5. **Start and Finish on Time** – As much as possible, get organized in advance and start on time. If you tend to start late, people will come late - or not at all.

6. **Be Brief** – Don't go into the gory details or drama of how you solved the problem or all the challenges involved. Five to eight minutes per story would be generous.

7. **Done** – Show only the work that is "Done Done", not "Done, But". If it isn't "Done" according to the team's definition of done, don't show it.

Sprint Retrospective

The final meeting in a sprint should be the Sprint Retrospective. It is during the Sprint Retrospective that the team focuses on inspecting and adapting the process they are using. This is perhaps the most important meeting of all since it is the opportunity for the team to pause, reflect on how they are doing and explore ways of improving.

Like all the Scrum meetings, the retrospective is timeboxed to 45 minutes per week of the sprint. So for a 2-week sprint, up to 90 minutes should be allowed.

Unlike the other Scrum meetings, the Scrum Master is responsible for facilitating the retrospective. For the other meetings, the Scrum Master is responsible to make sure they happen and are effective.

Another key difference between the retrospective and the other meetings is the participants. The retrospective is for the Scrum Team which means the developers, the Product Owner and the Scrum Master. The Scrum Team may invite others to participate, but there is no obligation to do that.

In practice I have seen teams that held their retrospective with the Product owner and others that did not. I prefer that the Product Owner be included since they have unique insights and sometimes have a different perspective on the sprint. Also, it is critical that the Product Owner function well for the team to be productive. So if there are issues with the Product Owner, they can be discussed in the retrospective. Unfortunately, if there are problems with the Product Owner it is unlikely that Product Owner is attending the retrospectives.

A key aspect of the retrospective is to come up with ideas for improvements. These improvement ideas are viewed as mini-experiments that can last a sprint or two. They are documented, action items are created, and they are tracked during the next sprint. It is this process of experimentation that provides a powerful mechanism for improvement. Since you are doing them every sprint, you have many opportunities to improve over the course of a year.

The most basic format for the retrospective is to address three questions:

What went well during the sprint?

What did not go well?

What do we need to improve?

Good Scrum Masters will quickly move beyond this format as they see that the retrospective yields less fruit over time. In fact, effective Scrum Masters will have a series of different techniques that they will use to generate insights and spark experiments to improve.

One of my favorite techniques was taught to me by Tom Cagley, an Agile and Software Development expert that I worked with for several years. The idea was to use a number of categories to spark thinking and brainstorming. As the facilitator, I would put the following 6 sticky notes on a whiteboard or flip charts and ask the team to silently brainstorm ideas within those categories: More, Less, Same, Enjoyable, Frustrating and Puzzling.

As the team had an idea or two, they would write them on a sticky note and place them on the board, announcing them as they went. One team member's idea would often spark someone else who would then write an idea. After about 5 minutes or so, the flow of ideas would slow or stop and we would move on to the next stage. The picture below shows one team's brainstormed ideas.

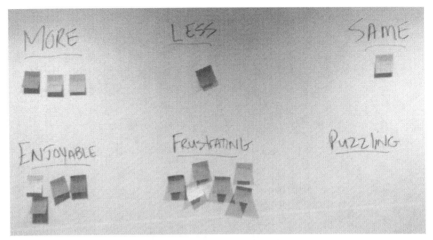

FIGURE 8. 9 - RETROSPECTIVE BRAINSTORMING TOOL

One problem you might have to deal with is when a team member or the entire team doesn't really invest in brainstorming. They might put one sticky note on the board, but not really try. In these cases, I announce that there is a quota of 5 (or 3, or 10) ideas per person. I literally count all the ideas and tell them if more are needed. It is helpful if this is done up front as it will usually result in better engagement.

After brainstorming, the next step is mute mapping, which is a form of affinity mapping done in silence. In mute mapping, the entire team goes to the board and begins to move similar ideas close together and dissimilar ideas far apart. They don't talk; rather, everyone engages to move the sticky notes around. As the groups of ideas begin to firm up, the Scrum Master or a team member names each of the clusters, based on the ideas.

Finally, the team uses dot voting to decide on which named cluster or clusters they want to focus on for the next sprint. Dot voting is a technique to get everyone involved in decision-making. Each team member is given a number of votes that they can use to pick the category. They can place all their votes on one item, or spread them around. To determine how many votes each person gets, take the total number of items, divide by 3 and then add one. So if there are 10 items, each team member would get (10/3 + 1) or 4 dot votes. The team members go to the board and put their votes by the items.

In the example shown below, the team ideas were clustered into refactoring, review and performance. Refactor and performance each got 7 votes so those were the items selected for focus.

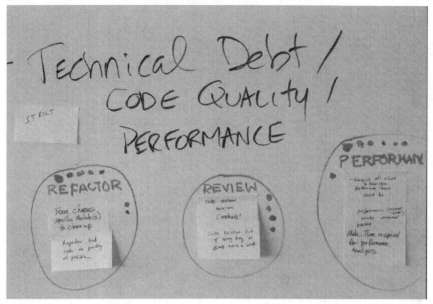

FIGURE 8. 10 - DOT VOTING

You may note that these techniques are expected to be done in silence. The idea here is to engage everyone in the process through parallel processing. What can happen when this technique is not used is that one person speaks, while everyone else listens or simply checks out. Left unchecked, one person can 'run the clock out' and exhaust all the time for the retrospective. His teammates may actually appreciate this if they don't really want to engage in the retrospective process! Scrum Masters need to use effective facilitation techniques to engage everyone and unleash the ideas and creativity from those that are vocal, as well as those that might be more reserved.

For more detailed information about retrospectives, I would recommend a couple of books. "Project Retrospectives", by Norm Kerth, is an excellent detailed description of how to run a retrospective and applies to the Agile Sprint Retrospective Meeting as well. One of the key techniques that I learned from a mentor was the use of Kerth's Prime Directive. By reading the following statement at the beginning of a retrospective, and getting everyone to verbally agree to it, you can put the team on solid footing for a candid discussion. If someone doesn't agree, then don't proceed with the retrospective.

"Regardless of what we discover, we understand and truly believe that everyone did the best job they could, given what they knew at the time, their skills and abilities, the resources available, and the situation at hand."

— Norm Kerth, Prime Directive (Kerth, n.d.)

Another excellent reference on retrospectives is Esther Derby's cleverly titled "Agile Retrospectives". One thing I like about this book is the plethora of tools that Esther introduces. Esther also provides a framework of distinct phases that are useful when applied to the retrospective: (Derby, 2006)

- Set the stage
- Gather data
- Gain insights
- Decide what to do
- Close the meeting

I like to plan my retrospective agenda using timeboxes for each of these phases. It helps me and it seems to help the team.

5 Tips for Effective Retrospectives

Here are some tips that I have found helpful when conducting retrospectives over the years.

1. **Retrospectives are owned by the team** – It is not open to outsiders, and the team decides what should be focused on.

2. **No Blaming** - Assume that everyone did their best given the circumstances. If possible, read Norm Kerth's "Prime Directive" aloud at the start of the iteration and ask for everyone to agree before proceeding.

3. **No Complaining** – Focus on what needs to improve, and how to improve it. Don't waste valuable time making excuses, justifying, or complaining.

4. **Pick One** – The general rule of thumb is to pick only one item to try to improve on each iteration. Doing more will dilute the team and nearly always result in less getting done. Add that

item as a user story, with tasks, to the backlog for the next iteration. Track that the user story gets completed, just like the other work in the iteration.

5. **Activities, Not Interviews** – Rather than the Scrum Master interrogating everyone to determine what could have worked better, get everyone involved using exercises such as silent brain storming, or having pairs or trios work on items. Regardless of the actual approach used, everyone should participate.

Other Scrum Meetings

There are a handful of other meetings that many Scrum practitioners and teams have found helpful. Though not considered official Scrum meetings per the Scrum Guide, many Scrum practitioners have come to recognize the need for some of these meetings and build them into their process.

Product Backlog Refinement

The most popular of these unofficial meetings is the Product Backlog Refinement meeting. This is sometimes called a grooming meeting, pre-planning, PBR, or simply refinement meeting. The purpose of the meeting is to reduce variability in the high priority backlog items, the ones that will be pulled into the next sprint or two.

Variability in the backlog affects both productivity and predictability. Teams can improve their productivity and predictability by taking on backlog items that are somewhat uniform in size and have been analyzed and are well understood. There is a cost for this reduction in variability and that cost is context switching in the current sprint. In order to refine the backlog for future sprints, the team takes their eyes off the backlog items that they are currently working on, and they temporarily focus on items that are prioritized for future sprints. While this seems to run counter to the Scrum process and the purposeful team focus, it is necessary as an investment in future productivity.

The actual refinement or grooming process entails taking backlog items and breaking them down, conducting sufficient analysis on the items, estimating them, developing specifications by example (SBE) for each item and creating acceptance criteria. The team takes the lead for backlog refinement and includes the Product Owner and other subject matter experts as needed.

There is a fair amount of variance in approach for the grooming process and refinement meeting. The Scrum Guide recommends that teams spend between 5 and 10% of their sprint time on refinement. This would be 4-8 hours for a 2-week sprint. I've worked with teams that had relatively consistent backlog items and they did little or no grooming. What refinement was completed, was primarily led by the Product Owner and one or two team members. It was not a full team activity.

On the other end of the spectrum was the process described by Craig Larman in my Scrum Master Certification training. Larman believes that the grooming process can only take place in the context of a full team meeting. A stickler for avoiding handoffs, Larman insists that all analysis needs to be completed during this meeting. He believes that maximum learning and group understanding comes from the discussions during the meeting, and strictly forbids bringing any type of requirements document in the meeting.

For those teams that need a more structured process, a 'definition of ready' can be applied to the refinement process. I recommend the definition of ready approach, and encourage teams to track readiness using a checklist.

Similar to the definition of done which serves as exit criteria for the sprint, the definition of ready represents entrance criteria for the sprint. It is a list of criteria that an item needs to meet to be deemed ready to be taken into a sprint. The lists of items below are things one might find on a definition of ready list:

- Estimated
- Broken down to 1/3 of the sprint or smaller
- Do all team members understand the item?
- Have acceptance criteria been developed?
- Is technical analysis required?

The definition of done could be written on a piece of flip chart paper and hung in the team area. I've also helped teams to create a tracking matrix on a piece of flip chart paper. The photo below shows how a team tracked story readiness using a flip chart. The backlog items are represented by the yellow sticky notes on the left column, and the 8 criteria that make a story ready are across the top. An item's readiness is represented by a small sticky note in the appropriate column. This approach provides a low-tech, but clear visual status of each item. This chart was hung in the team's workspace, and could easily be carried to another room if the backlog refinement meeting was conducted there.

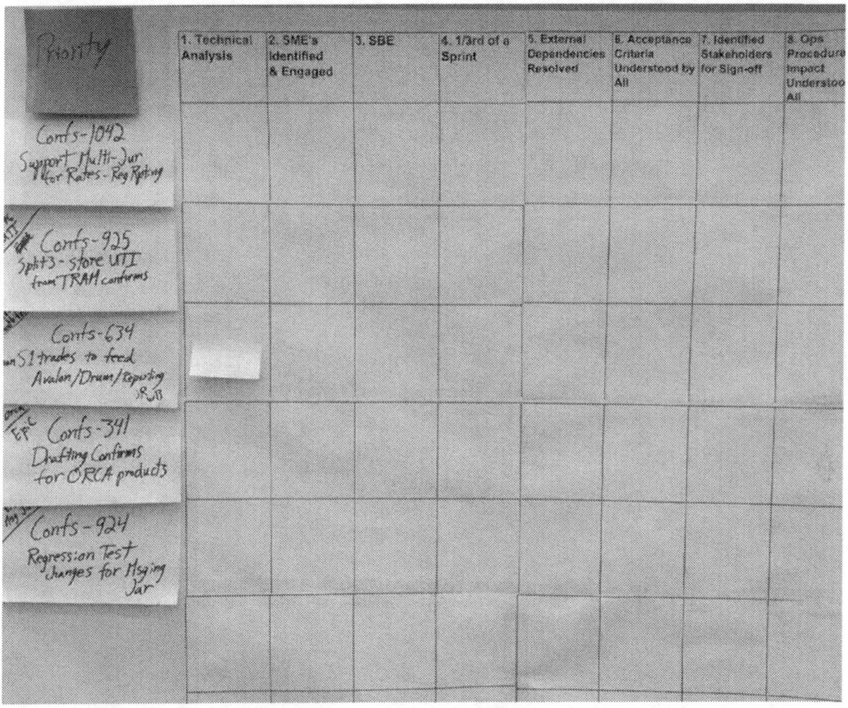

FIGURE 8. 11 - TRACKING STORY READINESS

Contrary to the approach recommended by Larman where the whole team does refinement, some teams have found that analysis is best done by team members whose primary skillset is business analysis or testing. They review the requirements and do some pre-digestion of those requirements, sharing their findings with the team.

For example, one team that I coached was responsible for understanding complex regulatory requirements and implementing solutions that met those requirements. The requirements were complex and often confusing or contradictory. Even the subject matter experts within the company lacked all the information needed by the team. For this team, they decided it made the most sense to have one team member specialize in these requirements. That one individual attended industry calls and worked closely with the SMEs available to determine the requirements. That individual then translated the requirements into specifications by example (SBE) and other documents that were discussed with the team. It was a concern to me as the coach that there was a specialist on the team, because this created a key man risk. The team mitigated this over time.

The cross functional team approach would have advocated that the specialist begin training others to become better at understanding and analyzing the complex requirements. They would actually refrain from performing their primary skill, while they taught others. It would be slower in the short run, but ultimately build capability for the team. It is up to each team to figure out the best approach for refinement.

The Product Backlog Refinement process works best if planned as a series of regular meetings that occur during the sprint. An agenda should be created for these meetings that include specific backlog items to be reviewed, based on the Product Owner's priorities. The discussions should be facilitated and timeboxed like the other Scrum meetings. If the items are reasonably sized, 20 minutes is a good starting point for a timebox for each item. At the end of the 20 minute timebox, the team can vote on whether to continue to discuss the item or move on to another.

The goal of the backlog refinement meeting is to have sufficient stories that are 'ready' for the sprint. If story readiness is a challenge, consider adopting some of the techniques in the preceding session to improve.

The Sprint

The Scrum Guide considers the Sprint itself an event, one that holds all the other events. I don't think it hurts to consider the Sprint an event, but it feels a little redundant.

The timebox for the Sprint is one month or less. These days, most teams use 2 weeks, though I have supported teams who have used 1-week, 3-week, and 4-week sprints. Shorter sprints tend to encourage more focus and sense of urgency and are recommended when teams are trying to be more disciplined and identify impediments. Longer sprints might be needed when teams have larger and more complex backlog items that cannot be broken down further. Longer sprints might also be appropriate when teams are struggling to deliver on the shorter sprints. That said, making a sprint longer will usually hide more problems than it solves so I rarely encourage a team to do that.

I often hear teams talk of the overhead associated with meetings and use that to argue for a longer sprint. With the exception of the daily standup, all the Scrum events are proportional in length to the sprint. So changing the sprint length doesn't have a meaningful impact.

Another argument for lengthening the sprint is that the team feels under pressure to deliver and doesn't get a break. This argument also falls apart under examination. The pace of work should always be constant and sustainable. If the team is feeling pressure, they can simply back off and take on fewer backlog items in each sprint.

Release Planning

Another unofficial Scrum meeting is release planning. The purpose of release planning is to create the high level backlog and timeline for the project, or at least the first release of that project. We covered release planning in detail in Chapter 5.

Schedule for the Meetings

Those new to Scrum often get alarmed at the number of meetings. It's a lot of meetings they contend. I agree! Meetings are a significant investment in team time and it is important that the time be used effectively. Each meeting has a purpose, expected participants, a timebox and an agenda. Rather than being a waste of time, Scrum meetings tend to be some of the most well organized meetings I've ever seen.

Additionally, if the Scrum process is working effectively, the team doesn't have many other meetings. They don't have status meetings and they don't get pulled in to many of the pointless other meetings that are held. They are able to focus on the backlog items for the current sprint.

As mentioned earlier, the recurring Scrum meetings tend to create their own predictable cadence or rhythm. That cadence provides a familiar and convenient structure so that meeting rooms and times can be scheduled in advance, and time is not lost booking rooms or rescheduling meetings around individual schedules. The distinct purpose and timing of the meetings allows the team to focus on one thing at a time.

From a calendar perspective, the meetings for a 2-week sprint or iteration might look something like the chart below.

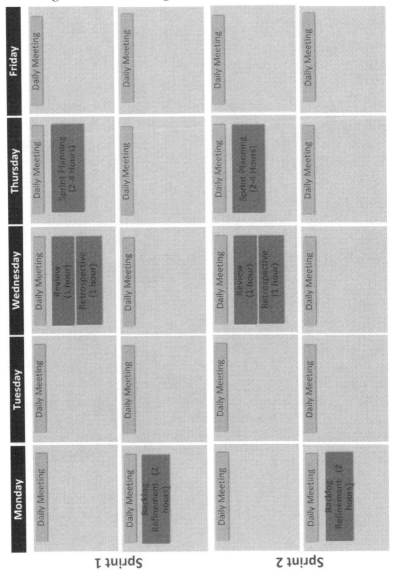

FIGURE 8. 12 - SCRUM MEETINGS IN A TWO-WEEK ITERATION

Summary of Scrum Meetings

The following chart provides a summary of the various Scrum meetings.

Meeting	Purpose	Attendees	Timebox for a 2-Week Sprint	Inputs	Outputs
Sprint Planning 1	Determine "What" will be in the sprint.	PO, Team and SM	4 hours for both Sprint Planning Meetings; generally 1-2 hours for SP1	Prioritized backlog, Definition of Done, Acceptance Criteria	Sprint Goal, Offer list from the PO
Spring Planning 2	Determine "how" to complete all the items.	Team, SM optional	4 hours for both Sprint Planning Meetings; generally 2-3 hours for SP2)	Product Owner Offer	Acceptance Email from the team, Tasks for all stories, Team Capacity, Burndown Chart, Task Board
Daily Scrum or Standup	Support Team Fine-grain coordination	Team, SM and Product Owner optional	15 minutes per day	Team activities	Team agreement on tasks to be worked next
Sprint Review	Team shows work completed and gets feedback or acceptance from the PO; inspect the product increment and adapts the product.	Team, PO, SM Optional	2 hours	Completed Items	Accepted backlog items. Revised Product Backlog.
Sprint Retrospective	Provide an opportunity for the team to inspect and adapt their processes.	SM, Team, Others by invitation	90 minutes		Identified improvements that are included in the next sprint backlog.

FIGURE 8. 13 - SCRUM MEETING SUMMARY

Chapter 8 Summary

- Scrum has pre-defined meetings that form a rhythm or team cadence. Each meeting has a purpose, attendees, timebox and expected outcomes.

Chapter 9: Scrum Artifacts

Key Takeaways for Chapter 9

By the end of Chapter 9, you will:

- Understand the role and importance of the Product Backlog
- Discuss in detail the composition of the Product Backlog, how it is created and some common backlog mistakes
- Introduce User Stories as a convenient way to state backlog items
- Discuss the Sprint Backlog and the Potentially Shippable Product Increment

Introduction

We have already introduced the Scrum artifacts in the previous units. These include the Product Backlog, Sprint Backlog and the Potentially Shippable Product Increment as shown in the diagram below. We will explore each of these in detail in the sections that follow.

FIGURE 9. 1 - SCRUM ARTIFACTS

The Product Backlog

The Product Backlog is probably the most important artifact, since it is the tool that drives development. It is through the Product Backlog that the Product Owner expresses the business needs and priorities. In fact, this is the most important role of the Product Owner – to make sure that the backlog is up to date, that it has been prioritized appropriately and that it is available to the team.

The Product Owner prioritizes the Product Backlog based on business value and return on investment. As noted in Chapter 7, the team will advise the Product Owner on prioritizing for risk and technical dependencies. Generally speaking, risky items are given a higher priority in the backlog than items that are not risky. In this way, the team reduces risk faster when they complete new features. The team also provides information on technical dependencies that the Product Owner may not know.

The team uses the Product Backlog as a queue for new features and product functionality. The team relies on this alone – they don't work from other lists, generate their own requirements, or take requests from others. Let's do a deep dive into Product Backlogs including the characteristics of a good backlog, an introduction to user stories and story format and the INVEST acronym. Let's also look at each Product Backlog item as representing a small vertical slice of functionality and discuss some common Product Backlog mistakes and then how backlogs are created.

In case it is not clear, there should be just one Product Backlog per product. Multiple teams can work on the same backlog, and one team can work on multiple backlogs (not recommended) but it would not make sense to have multiple backlogs for the same product.

DEEP Product Backlogs

DEEP is an acronym that is often used to describe a good Product Backlog. The D stands for Detailed. Product backlogs are sufficiently detailed in that it is clear what functionality is needed, or how the product should behave. This is where the Product Owner is able to express the business need in a way that is easy for the team to understand. It doesn't mean that the Product Backlog has implementation details, or describes how the team is to build it. There should not be a technology specification in the Product Backlog.

The level of detail will also be different for different backlog items. It is typical for a Product Backlog to be quite detailed for those items that are top priority and likely to be worked on in the near term. The lower priority items may be less detailed – this is shown in the diagram below. This helps reduce waste since some of the lower priority items may not be done, and even if they are done, it may be a while and the team might forget everything they discussed about the item. Or, the team may learn more about what is actually required.

The first E in DEEP is for Estimated. Everything in the Product Backlog should be estimated in story points. This supports release planning and provides the team and Product Owner some information on how long it would take to complete everything in the backlog. The total work remaining in story points and the time it should take the team to complete the backlog, based on velocity, should be readily computable at all times. This is not to say that everything in the backlog would be completed at some point – it almost certainly won't because of the next characteristics of backlogs.

The second E stands for Emergent. By emergent, we mean that the backlog items will change and evolve over time. The backlog is not considered static in any sense. Traditional projects will usually try to freeze or lock down requirements at the start of the project, where Agile teams benefit from letting the needs evolve based on feedback and learning. The Product Owner and team collaborate together to review and update the Product Backlog based on experience from the sprints, as well as what they learn about the product, customers and competitive environment. The backlog changes and emerges over time; some teams find that they can stop development and call the project "done" before all the backlog items are completed. The Product Owner is responsible for the return on investment (ROI) and should continually be evaluating how the remaining stories in the backlog will impact ROI.

The P in DEEP stands for Prioritized. The backlog should always be prioritized from top to bottom, with the most important features at the top. It is rank ordered. We don't use priority schemes like Low/Medium/High because that can lead to everything being designated as 'High', or people saying "everything has to get done". The team can only work on a few items at a time and the Product Owner supports this by rank ordering the Product Backlog.

I sometimes find it helpful to think of the Product Backlog as a pile of rocks that represent the individual backlog items as shown below. Though it doesn't reflect the rank ordering of the backlog, but it does demonstrate how the top priority items need to be well understood, small and detailed. The lowest priority items may be big, not well understood and simply placeholders for major pieces of work.

Top Priority Items
- Smaller
- Detailed
- Well understood

Low Priority Items
- Bigger
- Less detailed
- Not necessarily well understood

FIGURE 9.2 - DEEP PRODUCT BACKLOG

Size of the Product Backlog

"How big should our Product Backlog be?" is a question that I am frequently asked. "I don't know" is the answer that I usually give, followed by, "what are you working on?" I've worked with some teams who were doing true R&D and leveraged the "emergent" nature of the Product Backlog by keeping only 10-15 items in the backlog at any one time. I've worked with other teams that supported legacy applications that had a backlog of 700+ items!

A general rule of thumb is that the Product Backlog should have no more than 100 items. Larger than that, and it becomes nearly impossible for one person to prioritize the Product Backlog effectively. In the case of the team with 700+ maintenance items, a colleague of mine helped them to cluster similar requests, de-dupe and delete items that were more than a year old. Through this process, they were able to reduce the Product Backlog to about 80 items.

User Stories

Product backlog items are frequently stated as user stories, a concept that originated in Extreme Programming. A user story is a way of expressing the business need in a particular fashion – to answer the questions of who, what and why. Though many people use the concept of user stories, it is by no means required and it is not an official part of Scrum.

A handy way of thinking about the user story is the 3 C's; card, conversation and confirmation. In the early days of XP, user stories were written on physical note cards, either 3x5 or 4x6. The cards could be laid out on a table, they could be sorted and prioritized, and even be passed around and discussed in a meeting. Notes were jotted on the cards during discussions to remind the team of specific details about the story.

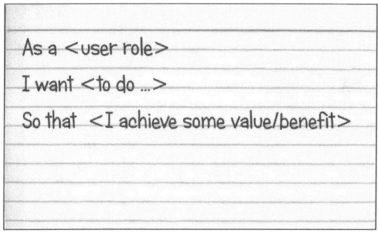

FIGURE 9.3 - USER STORY

One key benefit of the note card approach was that teams were forced to make stories very small in order to be able to put them on a card. It also prevented a lot of detail being recorded since there just wasn't much space for it. Other benefits of the card approach was that it was low cost and lightweight.

The second C of the user story represented "conversation". With Agile in general, and user stories in particular, the idea is to rely on discussions to get to a common understanding, and not on documentation. The card and user story were a reminder to have a conversation about the story. The Product Owner and team would meet and discuss the story; conversation largely replaced the detailed documents. Some teams may find it necessary to write something down, but many teams find documents unnecessary if they have small user stories and conversations with the Product Owner about the business need.

This is a big shift for many of us who have been involved with challenged or troubled projects and learned to document, document, and document some more. We believed that good requirements documents protected us from scope creep and virtually guaranteed that we would deliver what the end users wanted. Except that they didn't!

The final C represents confirmation. Confirmation means the test or acceptance criteria that will be used to determine whether we achieved the story or not. By beginning with the end in mind, we make sure we all agree on what we are going to build. Traditionally the acceptance criteria were written on the back side of the physical card.

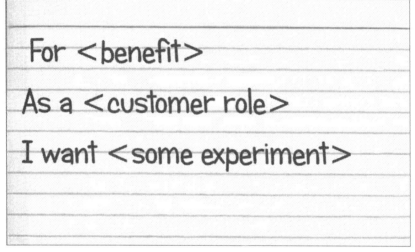

FIGURE 9. 4 - ALTERNATIVE USER STORY

The particular convention of the user story can vary. The format shown on the card above, "as a"…"I want"…"so that" was said to be developed at Connextra; it has been made popular by Mike Cohn and other Agile proponents. An alternative format recommended by Craig Larman is shown in the card at left. Larman contends that this format helps facilitate better conversations.

INVEST

There is another helpful acronym that relates to user stories. Bill Wake is credited with the creation of the INVEST mnemonic: (Wikipedia, 2014)

Independent – User stories should be independent of each other, as much as possible. That is, they can be moved around in the backlog and developed separately.

Negotiable – The user story should not represent a contract between development and the Product Owner. Rather, it should represent a business need, and the team can negotiate with the Product Owner on the best way to satisfy that business need.

Valuable – This probably goes without saying but each user story should deliver some value to the end user.

Estimable – Teams should be able to estimate the user story. If they cannot, the story is either unclear or too large.

Small (or sized appropriately) – User stories that are small are easier to plan, and lower risk. And as mentioned earlier, teams are more productive when stories are smaller and evenly sized.

Testable – The user story should be written in such a way that tests can be developed and the team can validate that the story has been developed correctly.

Thin Vertical Slices

Another aspect of user stories is that they represent a thin vertical slice of development that provides some value to the end user. If you look at the diagram of the slice of cake to the right, imagine a thin vertical slice of development that includes the UI and all the layers down to the database. That is how user stories should be developed. Features are built front to back, top to bottom in "thin vertical slices" to flush out risk and deliver business value early.

The alternative to this approach would be to work in horizontal layers, developing just the UI or just the application. The reason that this doesn't work is that you aren't delivering usable features or functionality in each sprint.

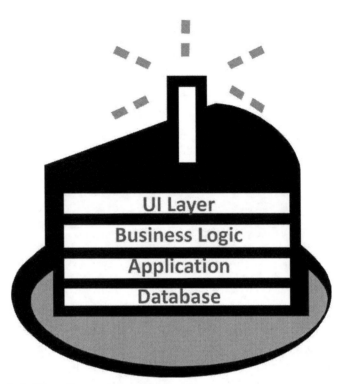

FIGURE 9. 5 - USER STORIES AS VERTICAL SLICES

Common Product Backlog Mistakes

Though the Product Backlog is a pretty simple concept, mistakes are not uncommon. Roman Pichler outlined the following Product Backlog mistakes in his excellent book, *Agile Product Management with Scrum.* (Pichler, 2010)

Disguised Requirements Specification

The disguised requirements spec is when we agree we won't do a specification, but we create that in the list of detailed and perfect stories created in advance. This is not emergent and the team doesn't get the benefit of learning about the product and getting feedback. It locks things in, prematurely. And it may reflect distrust or a high degree of separation among the team and the Product Owner.

Santa's Wish List

Similarly, the Santa's Wish List approach represents everything that anyone could possibly want. Like the previous approach, it is specified in advance and not emergent. It becomes difficult to prioritize and maintain, and learning and user feedback are not easily incorporated.

Requirements Push

With this approach, the Product Owner or SMEs supporting the Product Owner, develop requirements documents and toss them over the wall to the team. Rather than have conversations, there is a document handoff. It would be better to avoid the waste of writing the document, and just get the appropriate people in the room to have a conversation with the team. The team can then write whatever documentation is necessary.

Grooming Neglect

If the Product Owner doesn't stay on top of the backlog, duplicate or vague items begin to turn up and can slow down sprint planning meetings. A recent team I coached inherited a backlog of 300 items which is much too many to manage effectively.

Competing Backlogs

In an attempt to get the most out of people, some teams are asked to work on multiple backlogs at the same time. This runs counter to most of what Scrum encourages. Instead of working on multiple backlogs in the same sprint, Pichler recommends that teams focus for one or several sprints on one backlog, then shift gears and work on another backlog. I've also worked with Product Owners to combine those disparate backlogs into one prioritized list to eliminate the potential for conflicting priorities.

Where do Backlogs Come From?

While we have discussed what Product Backlogs look like and common mistakes to avoid, we have not looked at how to create a Product Backlog. We want to avoid the Christmas Wish List approach where we create a list of every possible item that could be built, for the reasons already mentioned. We also don't want to create a list of tasks that need to be done – the Product Backlog should be features and functions, or thin vertical slices of development.

If you are building a new application to replace an old one, there may be a temptation to simply rebuild all the functionality of the old system. This is rarely a good approach since it can lead to waste, and will just replicate whatever outdated business processes and thinking went into the old system. It would be better to use some form of 80/20 analysis to identify the key business activities that the old system supported, and then work with the Product Owner and end users to develop functionality that supports the optimal process.

Another approach that I have used with teams is to brainstorm, as a team, the key features and functions that are required for the product to be effective and deliver business value. We start with a high level view of the system and progressively break the features and functions down. You can generate a pretty good backlog of work in 15-20 minutes. It would then be up to the Product Owner to prioritize the list of items, and remove any that are not appropriate or desirable. Of course if the Product Owner already knows the features and functions, they could create the list on their own.

Another more structured approach to Product Backlog development is to use a use case diagram to identify major uses of the system. The use case diagram shows the system, and how actors interface with the system to do their work. As an example, consider Uber, the transportation application that has grown popular. A use case diagram for Uber might look like the one below. The diagram shows the actors, like the customer and taxi driver, and the various activities that each actor is trying to accomplish.

To create user stories, we start with one activity for one actor, and we breakdown the work into smaller items until we have a small slice of functionality. For example, for the Taxi Driver in the Use Case Diagram example below to "Accept a Fare", there are probably many individual user stories that would need to be completed to support the functionality.

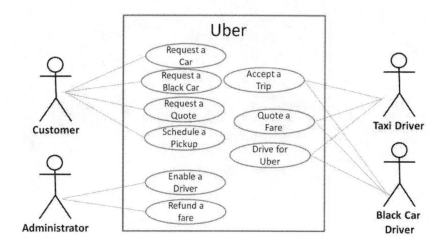

FIGURE 9.6 - USE CASE DIAGRAM

Another traditional approach to generating user stories is called story mapping. Story mapping starts with the business process. Each step of the process is laid out on a wall or white board using sticky notes. Then, the team works together to create user stories to support each of the steps. The diagram below shows the results of one such session. The purple notes across the top were the process steps, and the yellow steps across the bottom were user stories.

FIGURE 9.7 - STORY MAPPING

A relatively new approach that is gaining some traction in Agile circles is called Impact Mapping. With Impact Mapping, we start with our overall goals for the initiative, project or product, and then we use a very structured approach to identify activities and deliverables which might help us achieve those goals. It begins with identifying "Who", or the actors that can help us to achieve the goal. These may be end users, key business stakeholders, or customers. We then ask the question, how would each specific actor impact the goal? And then we look at the "what" or the deliverables needed to achieve or support the impact. The process is shown in the diagram below. (Adzic, 2012)

Goal? - Who? - How? - What?
(Actors)   (Impacts)   (Deliverables)

FIGURE 9.8 - IMPACT MAPPING

Each of those deliverables is treated like a small experiment that may or may not get us closer to the goal that we set. We prioritize the deliverables based on the likely contribution or impact it will have toward the goal. Those deliverables become Product Backlog items.

We can even use the thinking to easily map to the user story format as shown in the diagram below.

User Story Format:

As a <Who>
I Want <What>
So that <How>

FIGURE 9.9 – IMPACT MAPPING TO PRODUCT BACKLOG ITEMS

A key part of the experiment approach contained in Impact Mapping is the metrics. We need to establish metrics that track whether or not each experiment led us closer toward our goal, or moved us in another direction. Good metrics will tell the team whether they should keep going, or if they should pivot and go in another direction.

Tools for Product Backlogs

There are lots of tools on the market to help Product Owners manage the Product Backlog. Note that there is only one Product Backlog for the team – managing multiple lists in different tools is not effective. I encourage teams to use the simplest tool that gets the job done. For example, if everyone is working in the same area, you could work with physical note cards. They are lightweight and low cost and require no training.

The next step up from notecards, and a very common tool is Excel. Excel makes it easy to track specific information about each story, to sort and prioritize, to assign categories, etc.

One downside of Excel is that only one person can edit at a time. Because of this, some teams have found Google Docs an effective tool for backlog management.

Moving up the sophistication scale would be any of the common issue or incident tracking tools. Jira is one of the industry leaders in this category and they have built Scrum and Kanban tools on top of their ticketing system. These tools have the advantage of easily gathering backlog items, though that ease may be offset by the Product Owner's ability to see and prioritize that backlog.

Finally, there are tools built from the ground up to support Agile and Scrum. VersionOne and Rally are two of the leaders in this category.

Sprint Backlog

The second Scrum artifact is the Sprint Backlog. The Sprint Backlog is the subset of backlog items or stories that are selected for the sprint, along with the tasks necessary to complete those backlog items. The Sprint Backlog is specific to a sprint. It is created during sprint planning, and it represents all the work to be completed within the sprint.

The Sprint Backlog is reflected in the team's task board. In the picture shown below, the user stories are posted on the far left using orange sticky notes. The yellow sticky notes to the right of the stories represent the tasks needed to complete each of the user stories. As tasks are started and completed, they are moved from "To do" to "WIP" to "Done". All of the stories and tasks make up the Sprint Backlog.

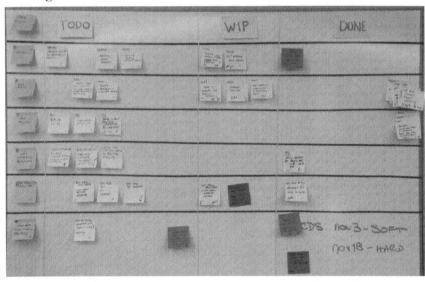

FIGURE 9.10 - A TEAM TASKBOARD

The Sprint Backlog is constantly updated to reflect the work that is in front of the team. New tasks may be discovered during the sprint and added to the Backlog. Tasks that are completed or discovered to be unnecessary are taken off the backlog. At the end of the sprint, the board is cleared.

During the sprint, the team only focuses on that work remaining to complete the sprint. It is irrelevant how much time was already spent or what tasks were already done. The team stays focused on completing the remaining Sprint Backlog within the sprint.

The Burndown Chart mentioned earlier is a helpful tool to compare remaining capacity with the remaining work. The team can use the Burndown Chart to confirm that they are on track or to determine that they need some extra focus or effort to get the work done. They might also see that it will not be possible to achieve all the work of the Sprint – in that case, they would notify the Product Owner that one or more backlog items will not be completed. It is much better for the team to get some backlog items completely done, rather than have most things 'almost done'.

As noted in Chapter 8 when we covered Sprint Planning 2, the team strives to take on only the amount of work that can be completed in the sprint. The team uses story points or hours to select an appropriate amount of work to be completed within the sprint. And this is important – it is up to the team to select the work that they will do. Once selected, only the team can change the Sprint Backlog. Managers, project managers and even the Product Owner are not allowed to add or delete work from the Sprint Backlog.

Potentially Shippable Product Increment

The final Scrum artifact is the Product Increment. Some people call it the Potentially Shippable Increment (PSI), or the Potentially Shippable Product Increment (PSPI). Jeff Sutherland calls it the Increment, and it represents the sum of all the Product Backlog Items completed during a sprint and all previous sprints. (Sutherland & Schwaber, 2011)

The key to the Increment is that the team adheres to their agreed "definition of done". This means that the Increment could be shipped if the Product Owner wanted to ship it. There is no additional work to be done on it – hence the reason many people add "Potentially Shippable" on the name. The Increment must be ready to ship and the Product Owner makes the decision on whether or not to ship it.

Chapter 9 Summary

- There are 3 key Scrum Artifacts: the Product Backlog, the Sprint Backlog and the Product Increment. Of these, the Product Backlog is the most important artifact since it is used to drive development.
- Product Backlogs should be DEEP: Detailed, Emergent, Estimated and Prioritized.
- The Product Backlog is rank-ordered from top to bottom, with the highest priority items at the top.
- User stories are a popular way of stating items in the Product Backlog, though they are not a formal part of Scrum.

Chapter 10: A Day in the Life of a Scrum Team

Key Takeaways for Chapter 10

By the end of Chapter 10, you will:

- Have a clear understanding what it is like for an Agile team to operate together
- Understand Scrum teams from a number of different perspectives
- Understand challenges that different teams face

Overview

The focus of this Chapter will be to explore in detail what it is like to be on a Scrum team. Every Scrum team is a little bit different in terms of personality, approach, challenges and even in the way that they use Scrum.

We are going to walk through a typical day for four different teams. By exploring several teams, you will gain a better understanding of some of the commonalities among teams, as well as the things that make them unique. Whether you have experience with Scrum teams or not, this review will provide you some perspective on a team's ability to leverage Scrum.

Some of the things we will learn include the characteristics of Scrum teams that we explored in Chapter 8:

- Cross functional
- Correct Team Size
- Full-time Assigned to One Team
- Co-Located
- Focused
- Self-Organizing

We will also look at how the team approached cross-training, the Scrum events, the company culture and their relationship with the Product Owner.

Arctic Deer

Team Overview

The Arctic Deer was a relatively mature and high-performing team, responsible for developing financial solutions in Java. There were five team members, whose primary skillset was Java development, and one whose primary skillset was testing and QA. The team strove for cross training and all team members rolled up their sleeves to do whatever needed to be done. For example, all team members participated in requirements discussions.

A team role called the "face" of the team was responsible for communications with the Product Owner and external stakeholders, as well as for updating the team's task board and burndown chart. The face was also responsible for preparing the change control forms needed for production release every two weeks.

The Arctic Deer were extremely nimble and released their code to production every two weeks, and sometimes more frequently. The development tools and environment were necessary to support these frequent releases. The tools and environment supported continuous integration and automated testing. The environment also tracked Chapter test coverage and test results, and supported code reviews when developers checked in their code. Without these tools, releasing to production every 2 weeks would be too painful and costly.

A key strength of the team was their diversity. There were men and women on the team. Two team members were from India, one from China, one from Australia and two who were born in the US. The most senior member of the team has over 30 years of development in the domain, while the most junior team member has less than 2 years. Three of the team members have one or more advanced degrees (one had 3 Masters Degrees!).

I observed this team over the course of a year. They liked to have fun and even created a team shirt that they all wore on the day of the production release. During this time, I saw them operate with and without a Scrum Master. While they sometimes seemed to push back on the formality and discipline of Scrum, for the most part they embraced the Scrum approach. They used a 2-week sprint length, and for the most part they kept the meeting times, though sometimes they moved Sprint Reviews to accommodate the Product Owner's schedule.

A key contributor to the success of this team was their proximity to the Product Owner. The team itself was co-located and sat within 25 feet of each other. The Product Owner was located in the same building, on another floor. This made face to face meetings easy and the norm, and helped forge a positive relationship. This was a huge benefit that this team had that many in the same organization did not have.

Day in the Life

A typical day for this team starts at 8am, when the first team members arrive and begin work. The daily standup is at 9am, so prior to the meeting the team was continuing to work on the items from the previous day. Most days everyone was on time for the daily standup, though occasionally a team member would come rushing in right at 9am so that they could be on time for the meeting. At 9am, the team was punctual about standing up and gathering around the task board. Each person would check in on their progress from the day before.

The line manager for the team participated in the daily meeting. He often moved the process along by asking people to check in, and then he would follow up with questions to get additional details. After everyone checked in, the line manager would frequently provide updates from his manager or other business news as appropriate. It was not uncommon for him to introduce new work to the team in the daily standup, independent of discussions with the Product Owner.

After the standup, the team members returned to their nearby workstations. The "face" of the team would often stay behind and make updates to the task board and the burndown to reflect the work remaining in front of the team. Since the team was co-located, the team was able to rely on these tools hanging in the team area, and did not have a need for any online tools.

At lunchtime, some team members would eat their lunch at their desk to save time. Others would head out together to grab lunch at a nearby restaurant. The same four team members had lunch together almost every day.

The team would frequently have scheduled meetings with the Product Owner to discuss requirements for user stories in the backlog. Some of the team members would attend those meetings while others would stay at their desks to complete other work. The Product Owner would come to a meeting room near the team to have a face to face discussion about the requirements. Often, one of the team members would take some notes about the requirements to post on the team wiki for that story. The Product Backlog itself is maintained by the Product Owner in an Excel spreadsheet that is kept on a drive.

Key Team Challenges

There is a famous line from Tolstoy's **Anna Karenina** about unhappy families that I think can be paraphrased and applied to teams.

"Every successful team is successful in the same way; every challenged team is challenged in its own unique way."

While it's not a law of Scrum, it is an interesting way to look at team challenges. Every team has challenges, and frequently the challenges are unique to the team. So where did the Arctic Deer struggle?

The main challenge for this team was that they were working in an environment that was not particularly welcoming to Agile and Scrum. I would liken the situation to a team of researchers living in a camp at the North Pole. For the researchers, the conditions within the camp are tolerable. However, there are many factors outside the camp that made it dangerous and nearly inhospitable. It was a wonder then to me that this team survived and thrived despite that environment. Let me explain.

All of the team members on this team reported to the same line manager. This line manager was an early champion of Agile, and he was the one who initiated the shift to Agile from traditional methods.

Unfortunately, this manager was also a traditional command and control manager. So while he appeared to be supportive of the team and their efforts to self-organize, he was in reality directing the team and held tight to the reins of power and control. He decided who was on the team, and he told the team what to do and how to organize. He would participate in the team's daily standups, ask questions and provide directions. He would frequently call team members into his office to provide direction or make changes to priorities.

Part of the reason for the line manager's behavior was fear. He reported to a functional manager who did not understand or appreciate Scrum and Agile, and just wanted the job done. The line manager was afraid of getting in trouble. He would often change priorities, redirect the team, or pull individuals off the team to work on special projects.

I have seen this sort of thing happen in other bottom-up Agile transformations. Lacking top down support, teams try to create their own safe and protected environment within the bigger and less friendly environment. They strive to be Agile and sometimes they do a pretty good job of it. Unfortunately, if the organization is not Agile, it is hard to operate in an agile way from the bottom up. It is particularly hard to change the organization.

Unfortunately, most bottom-up Agile transformations tend to fizzle out or become Agile in name only. Without organizational culture change and support for self-organizing teams, true Agile is not possible. This may be the ultimate fate of the Arctic Deer.

Team Mobility

Team Overview

Team Mobility was a team that developed mobile solutions for an online retail company. The team mission was to ensure the main company retail site worked well on mobile devices, and to explore and pioneer mobile capabilities.

The team consisted of four full-time team members: a full time iOS developer, a full time Android developer, a technical lead and another web developer. They also had a testing resource that was shared about 50% with another team. They were supported by a Scrum Master who supported two other teams.

There was very little focus on cross-training and learning within Team Mobility. For the most part the team members stuck to their own primary skillset, and did not attempt to teach or learn from each other. This decreased their flexibility, particularly because they were a small team.

One strength of this team was that they were co-located, with the exception of the tester and the Scrum Master who had desks in their functional department. All of their desks were near each other in a pod, without cubicle walls between them. All team members could easily speak to one another without leaving their desks, and osmotic communications happened naturally. Their task board was located on one side of their pod and team members could have the daily meeting without getting up from their desks. (I did encourage them to standup during the daily Scrum, only because it helped them focus on each other, rather than continuing to work on something else.)

This team enjoyed high morale and really seemed to enjoy working together. They were all very laid back and casual about the work. There was very little diversity; they were all guys, mostly around 30 years old, all from the same area of the country, with common interests.

The Scrum Master for the team was young and energetic, though he lacked experience in the role. He facilitated many of the meetings and had the team doing Scrum.

Day in the Life

A typical day for this team started at 8am when a few of the team members trickled in. They frequently socialized with each other as they logged in, and sometimes kept talking until the daily standup at 9:30am.

At the daily standup, the team would face the task board. Despite it being in their area, they would appear surprised by their tasks, which indicated that the team didn't rely on the task board throughout the day. As each person checked in, the other team members were frequently quite interested in some of the creative and exploratory work being done. This often led to side conversations and deep dives, and the daily meeting rarely was less than 15 minutes. The Scrum Master would often be gauging whether to call attention to the discussions or to let it go.

After the standup, some of the team members would continue socializing, while others got focused on the work. The Scrum Master would update the task board and the burndown chart for the team, then return to his desk or visit another team.

The team continued socializing and working over the course of the day. They had no set routine for lunch. Sometimes a few of them would go to lunch together while others brought their own lunch and ate at their desk. Other meetings throughout the day were rare; sometimes the VP of Development would come to their work area and sometimes the team would go to his office to meet. Otherwise, the team mixed work and socializing until they finished for the day.

Key Challenges

A key weakness of Team Mobility was the lack of a true Product Owner. The technical lead acted as the Proxy Product Owner and received a lot of direction from the PMO. This was efficient because the technical lead was part of the team, though it did not serve the team well from a strategic and business priority point of view. The team often struggled with priorities and shifted direction frequently. There was very little vision.

The team also struggled with discipline and somewhat reluctantly followed the Scrum events. I don't think they appreciated the idea of being self-organizing, largely because the culture of the organization was somewhat laid back, and few had any working experience anywhere else. So they weren't very motivated to self-organize. Rather, their attitude was something like, "whatever".

The size of the team was another challenge. With only four core team members and little cross-training, there were key man dependencies and capacity limitations. The team could mitigate that with cross-training, but that had not been a focus.

Another challenge for this team was that the team member who did testing reported to a separate organization, the QA team. While he supported the team and their efforts, his end of year performance review was completed by the QA Manager. It was a subtle point, but one that came through in behavior and conversations. The tester didn't share the team goals as much as he did those of the QA Team. And testing tended to come at the end of the process, as a way to "break the system", rather than as an integral team role.

Far Flung

Team Overview

The Far Flung Team was a distributed team that operated as part of a small software solutions company. I've included this team because they are unique – they deliver solutions to multiple external clients of the company they work for, they are small and they are distributed.

The Far Flung Team supported multiple customers, which posed a unique set of challenges. How could the team prioritize needs across multiple clients? They could dedicate the work of a sprint to one client at a time. That was difficult because some clients had major development needs and others were in maintenance mode and had small needs. What the team settled on was an approach to maintain separate prioritized backlogs for each client, but then pull them together in one combined backlog. They pulled from this combined backlog for each sprint. A client services manager served as proxy for the client Product Owners. The client services manager helped to prioritize the combined backlog for the team. It became very common for the team to deliver stories for multiple clients in the same sprint.

Like Team Mobility, the Far Flung Team is small by Scrum standards with only four full-time members and one half-time member. The team was supported by a Scrum Master who was shared with two other teams. This smallness was felt most in terms of team member specialization, as well as continuity and capacity when team members took vacations or holidays. Four of the team members were developers with similar skill sets, while the half time person focused on requirements and testing. The specialization was primarily around client accounts; there was usually just one developer who fully understood each client.

The Far Flung Team was also distributed and rarely had the opportunity to work together in the same space. Three of the team members were located in Chicago, one was in Milwaukee and one was located in France! The team dealt with this by using instant messaging and web conferencing tools during the working days of their sprints. Also, the team members in Chicago and Milwaukee would meet at the company offices for their beginning and end of sprint meetings, like Sprint Planning, Review and Retrospective. The team member in

France didn't have this luxury and had never met most of the other team members in person.

The team was also unique in that several of the team members were developers, but had other outside interests and treated the job as part time. Two of the team members played guitar in a band, which led to unconventional work hours and patterns.

Because of their diverse backlogs and their physical distribution, the team used Rally as an online Agile tool. The use of the Rally tool helped them to coordinate their efforts and have a common view of the work in the Sprint. They did not have a corresponding physical task board since no two people worked in the same place.

Day in the Life

A typical day for the team would start early for the team member located in France. Like another member of the team, he also worked as a musician. His performances sometimes kept him up late so it was not a problem for him to sleep in a little, and shift his work day to align with other team members. He would often develop things early in the day and send them over to other team members to review or test.

Next up was one of the Chicago-based team members who was an early riser. He and his European counterpart would use Jabber and Skype to connect and collaborate. Another team member would work from the company offices and join the IM conversations when she arrived. The last team member to arrive was another musician in the group. He often showed up at his computer at home right at 10:00am in time for the daily Scrum meeting.

The daily meeting at 10 would generally flow pretty smoothly from day to day. These meetings usually took 20-25 minutes, which is beyond the 15 minutes that Scrum allows. Each person would bring up the task board in Rally and provide updates to their tasks, including changing the hours remaining or dragging the task to another column to change the progress. In addition to task status, team members shared updates from the clients as appropriate, since some of the team members were the point of contact for clients.

The rest of the day would be pretty quiet, with some IM conversations, and occasionally a phone call or Skype call. Calls frequently revolved around specific functionality for a particular client and the client services manager would schedule client resources to participate as appropriate.

As mentioned above, the team would all meet in the Chicago office for end and beginning of sprint meetings (except for the French team member). The team would do the review to the internal client engagement manager, their Scrum Master, and other members of the company's management team. There would frequently be other reviews scheduled with clients to go through a story, but this was more common mid-sprint or after the end of the sprint. After the Sprint Review, the Scrum Master would facilitate the team retrospective. This would be over a teleconference with a screen sharing tool for the team member in France. Then the team would break for lunch.

After lunch, the team would perform Sprint Planning. This generally lasted 3 hours and sometimes was not entirely completed. The team in the Chicago office bid farewell and did not see each other for another 2 weeks.

Key Challenges

The key challenges for this team were the physical separation and the team size. The distance made it difficult for effective team building and self-organization. The team performance was hindered by lack of growth and a fair amount of storming was common.

For example, the team had found it easier to divide and conquer rather than collaborate on stories. This meant that one team member was frequently responsible for each story, and for each customer. For the highest performing team members this did not cause a problem. It did cause a problem for the most junior developer who frequently did not finish the stories he committed to complete. He was reluctant to ask for help or let others know he was in trouble.

The physical separation made communications more difficult and disconnects were common. It was not uncommon for a client to complain about communication gaps between team members. This was somewhat mitigated by the fact that each Client had a developer that understood them and was their single point of contact. However, communications were less than perfect and the team struggled when members were on vacation.

The physical separation also hindered cross-training. There was virtually no pairing and little development of the more junior developers. The team worked in silos.

The team size was another challenge for Far Flung. Having just four and a half team members is below the recommended Scrum team. Compounded by the physical separation, this created problems with specialization, and key man risks for specific client accounts.

OmniPotent

Team Overview

The OmniPotent Team had a high degree of self-organization and consistent performance. I had a great relationship with this team over the year that I coached them, and I remain in contact with team members even though I no longer coach at this organization.

The OmniPotent Team was diverse, co-located, cross-functional and highly motivated. Most team members had Java development as their primary skillset, though one of them came from a testing and quality assurance background and had testing as their primary skillset. They were also very diverse: 3 team members were from India, one was from China, and 2 were from Chicago. A couple of the team members had over 20 years of experience in the same organization, while a few had 5 years of experience and one was a recent college new hire. Despite their background and primary skillset, everyone was willing to take on any task in the backlog, and they worked closely together teaching each other what they knew about the business and the legacy technologies. It was common for me to walk by their team space and see 2 or 3 clusters working together to develop the solution.

The team had good morale and enjoyed working with one another. I would frequently see them working late in the day, and they had occasional get-togethers outside work.

Unlike many Scrum teams, OmniPotent did not expect the Scrum Master to be a mini-project manager. They shared the Scrum Master with two other teams. The Scrum Master facilitated the retrospective, but otherwise rarely attended team meetings.

OmniPotent used a rotating team role called the information officer to keep them organized. Some of the key responsibilities of the information officer were:

- Make sure Scrum Meetings were set up for 2-3 sprints out
- Act as the single point of contact for the Product Owner and external stakeholders
- Maintain the team wiki page, task board and burndown charts throughout the sprint

Day in the Life

A typical day for OmniPotent started at 8am. They would frequently have a 2-hour Product Backlog refinement meeting scheduled at this time with their India counterpart and the subject matter experts in London. The team held their meetings from their desk using WebEx and web cameras, which helped them to connect and relate to the SMEs and the India team. It also reduced (though did not eliminate) their tendency to multi-task and do other work during the refinement discussion.

One team member, usually the information officer, would take the lead on facilitating the Product Backlog Refinement Meeting. The SME for this team would usually share their laptop screen, and bring up the user stories under discussion. They worked from a team wiki, including for their Product Backlog. They would work through each story, and refer to their team definition of ready for the story to make sure it was truly ready for the sprint.

The team included specification by example (SBE) in their definition of ready, so this was usually done during the Product Backlog Refinement Meeting. Typically a team member would create an SBE shell in Excel, and then work through the test conditions or specifications with the SMEs. By working together on refinement with the team in India, both teams understood all the items in the Product Backlog, which provided a lot of flexibility and additional capacity.

Once they concluded their Product Backlog refinement meeting, they often took a short break. Some team members would go to the lobby for Starbucks. Then they would meet at the task board at 10:30 for their daily Scrum meeting.

This team used a basketball as a talking totem as a way to focus discussion in the daily standup. They would stand near their task board, and take turns checking in on the 3 Scrum questions. The basketball was mostly effective, though one team member frequently interrupted or asked questions. The Scrum Master did not always attend the daily Scrum; when he did, he would sometimes try to re-focus the team or draw attention to the team member's behavior. Unfortunately, even with that focus the behavior didn't change much over time.

After the daily standup, the team would often split up in pairs and begin working on tasks from their board. It was more common for the team to pair than for them to work individually. Team members frequently went to lunch together, and then came back and spent the day pairing on the work to be completed.

Key Challenges

Geographic and time zone challenges were prevalent issues for the OmniPotent Team. While the team itself was co-located, they worked within an ecosystem that included another team and stakeholders who were not co-located. They worked against the same backlog as another development team in India who was 10.5 hours ahead.

The two teams shared responsibility for production support, and had to work through challenges and organization of that support. The teams also had shared meetings that they attended together, making scheduling harder and reducing flexibility. The teams had to negotiate times when they could both meet with the Product Owner for Sprint Planning 1, and Sprint Review, and the Product Owner was 2 hours behind the US team, and 12 ½ hours behind the India team. They also scheduled joint Product Backlog Refinement meetings with the India team and appropriate subject matter experts. For the most part, the team in India took on the brunt of the time zone pain, staying in their offices until 8 or 9pm at night.

Another key challenge for this team was the relationship with the Product Owner. The Product Owner worked in a different location, with a 2-hour time difference. The team never met the Product Owner face to face, and had not established a rapport with her.

Finally, another key challenge for the team was productivity. The team never tried to push or increase their productivity. Instead they tended to manage productivity so that they kept expectations low. Over the first 4-5 sprints, the team increased their productivity significantly as they worked through the mechanics of Scrum. Over the next 8 months, the velocity was pretty much flat. One team member verbalized this by saying they didn't want to over promise. It seems that the entire team colluded together to keep a constant pace, without pushing each other to increase their productivity.

Chapter 10 Summary

This Chapter provided an overview of what it is like to work in a Scrum team, based on the examples of several very different Scrum Teams. Each team was different in the overall organization they worked in, the way they applied Scrum and their approach to solve their unique challenges. Some teams were more productive than others, but all shared a common framework for improvement.

Appendix A – Glossary of Agile Terms

Affinity Estimating

A method of estimating a large number of items quickly, in parallel, using groups of similar items. Sometimes referred to as T-Shirt sizing.

Agile Project Leader

A Scrum Master, program manager, or other leader who is focused on supporting an Agile project, or a project in an Agile environment.

Burndown Chart

A visual tool for measuring and displaying team progress. The most common burndown chart represents remaining work in hours over an iteration for one team. Burndown or Burnup charts may also be used to measure the progress of completion of user stories at an iteration or release level.

Daily Scrum / Daily Meeting / Daily Standup

A short team meeting that happens at the same time every day and should last 15 minutes or fewer. The meeting is designed to allow the team to coordinate their efforts, and plan their days based on the flow and challenges of the development process. Each team member should answer 3 questions: what did I do yesterday, what am I planning to do today and what impediments do I currently have?

Definition of Done (DoD)

The team's agreement on what constitutes done for a user story, an iteration or a release. This agreement determines the tasks that the team needs to do to consider something done. The Definition of Done should match organizational standards.

Definition of Ready (DoR)

The team's agreement on the characteristics of a user story that would make it ready to bring into a sprint to be worked on. User stories are made ready during backlog refinement or grooming sessions which take place in advance of the sprint the items will be completed in.

Done

Sometimes referred to as "Done Done", this term is used to describe all the various tasks that need to happen before a story is considered potentially releasable. See Definition of Done.

Dot Voting

A facilitation technique used to quickly get agreement on top priorities or to select a subset of items to be focused on. Each person gets a set number of votes that they can use on one or multiple items. They vote by putting a dot using a marker on the whiteboard.

Empirical Process Control

Used with processes that are highly variable and unpredictable. It is based on inspecting the results of the process and making regular adjustments. It is often contrasted with predictive approaches which assume results can be predicted.

Epic

A very large user story that is eventually broken down into smaller stories.

Estimation

The process of agreeing on a size measurement for the stories, as well as the tasks required to implement those stories, in a Product Backlog.

Hardening Sprint

A sprint where functionality is not delivered, but testing, training, or other work is done. Generally, hardening sprints should be avoided as they represent risk.

Learning Debt

Similar to technical debt, learning debt is the accumulated cost of not learning in the organization. Includes not learning about the business, not learning about existing systems and not learning about new technologies among other things.

MMF (Minimal Marketable Feature)

The smallest prioritized chunk of customer-valued functionality that can be delivered.

MVP (Minimum Viable Product)

A version of the product which has just those features that allow the product to be deployed, and no more.

Osmotic Communications

With osmotic communication, teams that are seated together in the same room are able to pick up relevant information from overhearing conversations. It is as though they are learning by osmosis.

Pair Programming

An practice from XP where two programmers work together at one workstation. One types in code while the other reviews each line of code as it is typed in. The person typing is called the driver. The person reviewing the code is called the observer (or navigator). The two programmers switch roles frequently.

Pairing

A variation of pair programming where two people work together. This could include cross-functional (tester and developer), or even within the same discipline (analyst + analyst). Benefits include knowledge transfer, defect reduction and team-building.

Planning Poker

A consensus-based technique for estimating based on relative size of user stories. It is based on the wideband Delphi technique which uses crowd-sourcing to develop more consistent and accurate estimates of work.

Potentially Shippable Increment (PSI or PSPI)

PSI - Potentially Shippable Increment, PSPI stands for Potentially Shippable Product Increment, the small vertical slice of functionality that results from each sprint or iteration of an Agile project.

Product Backlog

A rank ordered list of the user stories that serves as the product or project requirements. The Product Backlog is maintained by the Product Owner.

Product Backlog Item

An individual feature or function for the solution. User stories are one format for a Product Backlog item.

Product Owner

A member of the Scrum team who represents the voice of the customer and is accountable for ensuring that the team delivers value to the business. The Product Owner writes customer-centric items (typically user stories), prioritizes them, and adds them to the Product Backlog.

Refactoring

An XP technical practice. It is the process of improving software design, without changing the functionality.

Retrospective

A Scrum team meeting that happens at the end of every development iteration to review lessons learned and to discuss how the team can be more efficient in the future. It is based on the Scrum principles of inspect and adapt.

Scrum

A development framework developed by Ken Schwaber and Jeff Sutherland which is used to address complex adaptive problems, while productively and creatively delivering products of the highest possible value. It is based on the adaptive and iterative methodology of software development. The name was taken from the game of rugby.

Scrum Master

A role on the Scrum team with accountability for removing impediments to the team's ability to deliver the sprint goal/deliverables. The Scrum Master is a servant leader. The Scrum Master ensures that the Scrum process is followed by the team, and they protect the team and keep them focused on the tasks at hand.

Servant Leader

A leader whose natural tendency to serve others first, which translates to a conscious choice to aspire to lead. The servant leader shares power, puts the needs of others first and helps people develop and perform as highly as possible.

Specification by Example (SBE)

A method of producing living requirements for a project which can be translated into automated acceptance tests (ATDD).

Spike

A user story that represents a short, time-boxed piece of research, usually technical, on a single story that is intended to provide just enough information that the team can estimate the size of the story.

Sprint (also called Iteration)

A fixed duration period of time where user stories are chosen to work on. The term Sprint comes from the Scrum methodology and is analogous to the term Iteration. A sprint is defined as a 2-4 week increment of software development activities that delivers working software and the end of the increment. External influences are not allowed to change the requirements of the stories being worked on.

Sprint Backlog (also called Iteration Backlog)

The work that the team commits to completing during Iteration Planning, which occurs at the beginning of each sprint. These are the backlog items that the team will deliver as well as all the tasks needed to complete those backlog items.

Sprint Planning (also called Iteration Planning)

A key Scrum meeting that occurs at the start of each iteration. The meeting is in two parts; during the first part of this meeting, the Product Owner describes the highest priority features to the team as described on the Product Backlog. In the second part of the meeting, the team then agrees on the number of features they can accomplish in the sprint and plans out the tasks required to achieve delivery of those features.

Sprint Planning Meeting

One of the key Scrum ceremonies where sprint planning occurs.

Sprint Retrospective Meeting

One of the Scrum Meetings that is held at the end of each iteration, this serves as an opportunity for the team to inspect and adapt their processes.

Sprint Review

One of the Scrum Meetings that is held at the end of each iteration, this serves as a brief review of the solution developed in the previous Sprint. Solution is reviewed and marked complete, and if necessary new backlog items are added.

Story Points

A relative measure used by Agile teams to represent the complexity and size of a user story. Points are used to provide a relative measure between two user stories, and cannot be compared between two teams.

Swarming

The process where all team members work together to move items to done in the shortest possible time. Team members focus on the items in priority order and pile on to get things done.

Task

A user story can be broken down in to one or more tasks. Tasks are estimated in hours during iteration planning, and then re-estimated daily once a team member begins working on them.

Taskboard

A form of visual management. It is generally a wall chart with cards and/or sticky notes that represents all the work (user stories and tasks) for a given iteration. The notes are moved across the board to show progress.

Team

In Scrum, the team is a cross-functional and self-organizing group responsible for delivering the product. A team is typically made up of 5–9 people who do all the actual work needed to be done with a particular piece of functionality (analyze, design, develop, test, technical communication, document, etc.).

Technical Debt

This is the consequences of poor or evolving software architecture and software development within a code base. Technical debt can be thought of as work that needs to be done before a particular job can be considered complete. It is relevant because of the cost and risk of making changes to products with high technical debt.

Timebox

A timebox is a set period of time to complete a meeting, task or activity. In Agile, the iterations are timeboxes that are the same length.

User Story

A very high-level definition of a requirement, containing just enough information so that the team can produce a reasonable estimate of the effort to implement it. A user story tells the who, what and why, in the everyday or business language of the end user. A user story is not intended to be exhaustive, or a substitute for conversation; in fact, it is considered a reminder to have a conversation between the users and the team. XP just uses the term "stories".

Velocity

A relative number which describes how much work the team can get done in story points over a period of time.

WIP

Represents any work that has been started but has yet to be completed. Incomplete work is one of the 7 Lean Wastes. Agile teams strive to minimize work in progress so that they maximize throughput.

Appendix B: Works Cited in this Book

Adzic, G., 2012. *Impact Mapping: Making a big impact with software products and projects.* s.l.:Provoking Thoughts .

Anon., 2014. *Agile Software Development.* [Online] Available at: http://en.wikipedia.org/wiki/Agile_methodology [Accessed 8 February 2014].

Anon., n.d. [Online] Available at: http://upload.wikimedia.org/wikipedia/commons/9/91/Fred_Broo ks.jpg [Accessed 03 December 2013].

Augustine, S., 2005. *Managing Agile Projects.* s.l.:Prentice Hall.

Beck, K. w. A. C., 2005. *Extreme Programming Explained: Embrace Change (2nd Edition).* Boston: Addison-Wesley.

Brooks, F. P., 1995. *The Mythical Man Month: Essays on Software Engineering, Anniversary Edition (2nd Edition).* s.l.:Addison-Wesley Professional.

Cockburn, A., 2007. *Agile Software Development: The Cooperative Game (2nd Edition).* s.l.:Pearson Education.

Cockburn, A. & Williams , L., 2000. *The Costs and Benefits of Pair Programming,* Salt Lake City, UT: s.n.

Cohn, M., 2006. *Agile Estimating and Planning.* s.l.:Pearson Education.

Cohn, M., 2009. *Succeeding with Agile: Software Development Using Scrum.* s.l.:Addison-Wesley Professional.

Cohn, M., 2012. *Agile Succeeds Three Times More Often Than Waterfall.* [Online]
Available at: http://www.mountaingoatsoftware.com/blog/agile-succeeds-three-times-more-often-than-waterfall
[Accessed 19 12 2013].

Collins, J., n.d. *Good to Great.* s.l.:s.n.

Cunningham, W., 2001. *The Agile Manifesto.* [Online]
Available at: http://agilemanifesto.org/
[Accessed 08 12 2013].

DeCarlo, D., 2004. *eXtreme Project Management: Using Leadership, Principles, and Tools to Deliver Value in the Face of Volatility.* s.l.:Jossey-Bass.

DeMarco, T. a. L. T., 1999. *Peopleware; Productive Projects and Teams.* s.l.:Dorset House Publishing Company.

Derby, E., 2006. *Agile Retrospectives: Making Good Teams Great.* s.l.:Pragmatic Bookshelf.

Highsmith, J., 2002. *Agile Software Development Ecosystems.* s.l.:Pearson Education Inc..

Highsmith, J., 2005. *Agile Declaration of Interdependence.* [Online]
Available at: Source http://pmdoi.org/index.html
[Accessed 09 12 2013].

Highsmith, J., 2010. *Agile Project Management: Creating Innovative Products.* s.l.:Addison-Wesley.

Hohmann, L., 2007. *Innovation Games; Creating Breakthrough Products Through Collaborative Plan.* s.l.:Addison-Wesley.

Kerth, N., n.d. *Project Retrospectives.* s.l.:s.n.

Larman, C., 2004. *Agile & Iterative Development.* s.l.:Addison-Wesley.

Larman, C. & Vodde, B., 2009. *Scaling Lean & Agile Development: Thinking and Organizational Tools for Large-Scale Scrum.* Boston: Pearson Education, Inc..

Moore, G. A., 1999. *Crossing the Chasm.* s.l.:HarperCollins.

Pichler, R., 2010. *Agile Product Management with Scrum.* Boston, MA: Pearson Education Inc..

PMI, 2015. PMI Fact File. *PMI Today January 2015.*

Poppendieck, M. a. T., 2007. *Implementing Lean Software Development: From Concept to Cash.* Boston, MA: Pearson Education, Inc..

Project Management Institute, 2008. *A Guide to the Project Management Body of Knowledge (PMBOK® Guide) - 4th Edition.* s.l.:Project Management Institute (PMI).

Rico, D., Sayani, H. H. & Sone, S., 2009. *The Business Value of Agile Software Methods: Maximizing ROI With Just-in-time Processes and Documentation.* s.l.:J. Ross Publishing.

Royce, D. W., 1970. Managing the Development of Large Software Systems. *Proceedings, IEEE WESCON,* pp. 1-9.

Standish Group, 2012. *Chaos Studies,* s.l.: s.n.

Sutherland, J., 2 Apr 2012. *The Scrum Papers; Nuts, Bolts, and Origins of an Agile Framework.* [Online] Available at: scruminc.com/tl_files/scrum_inc/documents/ScrumPapers.pdscruminc.com/tl_files/scrum_inc/documents/ScrumPapers.pdf [Accessed 01 04 2013].

Sutherland, J., Schoonheim, G. & Rijk, M., 2009. *Fully Distributed Scrum: Replicating Local Productivity and Quality with Offshore Teams,* s.l.: s.n.

Sutherland, J. & Schwaber, K., 2011. *The Scrum Guide: The Definitive Guide to Scrum: The Rules of the Game.* s.l.:Scrum.org.

Takeuchi, H. a. I. N., 1986. The New New Product Development Game. *Harvard Business Review.*

VersionOne, 2013. *The 7th Annual Survey of Agile Development,* s.l.: VersionOne.

Visitacion, M., 2011. *The PMO in an Agile World: Can't We All Just Get Along?,* s.l.: Forrester.

Vogt, E., n.d. *The Art and Architecture of Powerful Questions.* [Online] Available at: http://www.javeriana.edu.co/decisiones/PowerfulQuestions.PDF [Accessed 26 Mar 2014].

Wikipedia, 2012. *Empirical process (process control model).* [Online] Available at: http://en.wikipedia.org/wiki/Empirical_process_(process_control

model)
[Accessed 19 March 2014].

Wikipedia, 2014. *Code refactoring.* [Online]
Available at: http://en.wikipedia.org/wiki/Code_refactoring
[Accessed 24 February 2014].

WikiPedia, 2014. *Extreme Programming Practices.* [Online]
Available   at:
http://en.wikipedia.org/wiki/Extreme_programming_practices
[Accessed 24 February 2014].

Wikipedia, 2014. *INVEST (Mnemonic).* [Online]
Available at: http://en.wikipedia.org/wiki/INVEST_(mnemonic)
[Accessed 13 April 2014].

Wikipedia, 2014. *Plannign Poker.* [Online]
Available at: http://en.wikipedia.org/wiki/Planning_poker

Wikipedia, n.d. *Agile Management.* [Online]
Available at: http://en.wikipedia.org/wiki/Agile_management
[Accessed 04 Feb 2014].

Womak, J. e. a., 1990. *The Machine that Changed the World.* s.l.:s.n.

Appendix C – Recommended Reading list for Scrum Masters

Agile Coaching, by Rachel Davies and Liz Sedley

Agile Estimating and Planning, by Mike Cohn

Agile Product Management with Scrum: Creating Products that Customers Love, Roman Pichler

Agile Retrospectives, by Esther Derby and Diana Larsen

Bridging the Communication Gap: Specification by Example and Agile Acceptance Testing, by Gojko Adzic and Marjory Bisset

Coaching Agile Teams: A Companion for ScrumMasters, Agile Coaches, and Project Managers in Transition, by Lyssa Adkins

Collaboration Explained: Facilitation Skills for Software Project Leaders, by Jean Tabaka

Drive: The Surprising Truth About What Motivates Us, by Daniel H. Pink

Extreme Programming Explained: Embrace Change, Kent Beck

Implementing Lean Software Development: From Concept to Cash, Mary Poppendieck

Kanban, by David Anderson

Leading Self-Directed Work Teams, by Kimball Fisher

Management 3.0, by Jurgen Appelo

Project Retrospectives: A Handbook for Team Reviews, by Norman L. Kerth

Punished by Rewards: The Trouble with Gold Stars, Incentive Plans, A's, Praise, and Other Bribes, by Alfie Kohn

Scaling Lean & Agile Development, by Craig Larman

Succeeding with Agile, by Mike Cohn

The Five Dysfunctions of a Team, by Patrick Lencioni

The Machine that Changed the World, James P. Womack, et al

The Power of Appreciative Inquiry: A Practical Guide to Positive Change, by Diana Whitney, et al.

User Stories Applied, by Mike Cohn

Made in the USA
San Bernardino, CA
19 September 2015